GUIDE TO BETTER GARDENING

GALAHAD BOOKS

ANNUALS, PERENNIALS, BIENNIALS

Editor: Margaret Verner
Dust Jacket designed by Roswita Busskamp

Annuals, Perennials, Biennials published by
Galahad Books Inc., New York City.

This edition published by arrangement with
'Round the World Books Inc., New York, N.Y.

Library of Congress Catalog Card Number: 79-56674

ISBN: 0-88365-435-0

Printed in the United States of America.

PICTURE ACKNOWLEDGEMENTS:

All-America Selections Inc.: 17T, 18, 30, 71, 72, 74, 75T, 76T, 77T, 78T, 81 — Bodger Seed Co.: 10, 14, 15, 17B, 20, 21, 22T, 60, 61T, 62T, 63, 66B — Bristol Nurseries Inc.: 29, 31, 37T, 37B, 38, 46T, 51 — C.A. Best, M.A., Georgetown, Ontario: 85B, 87T — Ferry Morse Seed Co.: 22B, 32, 34L, 65T — George J. Ball Inc.: 39T, 66T — Keith Seed Co.: 57R — Lewis J. West, Wilmette, Ill.: 91TL, 91TR, 91B, 92T, 92B, 93T, 93B — Noweta Gardens, St. Charles, Minn.: 70, 73, 75B, 76B, 77B, 78B, 79T, 79B, 80T, 80B, 88 — Ontario Agricultural College: 50T, 83T — Pan American Seed Co.: 7, 19, 23B — Royal Botanical Gardens: 34TR — Schreiner's Gardens, Salem, Oregon: 40, 41L, 41R, 44B, 45T, 52, 82, 90 — Sheridan Nurseries: 34BR, 35L, 36B, 48L, 48R, 50B — Stokes Seed Co.: 6, 9T, 9B, 13, 23, 55, 56T, 57L, 59, 64T — W. Atlee Burpee Seed Co.: 5, 8, 12, 16, 24T, 24B, 25, 26T, 26B, 27L, 27R, 28, 35R, 42, 53, 54, 58, 67T, 67B, 68T, 68B, 89, 94T, 94B, 95 — Walter Marx Gardens Inc.: 36T, 43, 45B, 46B, 47, 49, 83B, 84, 85T, 86, 87B, 96.

Table of Contents

ANNUALS

ANNUALS

Annuals are an inexpensive way to landscape.

Landscaping with annuals

With the recent expansion of cities, more families are moving into newly-built homes in the suburbs. Once the actual moving is finished and they are settled, the next job to face is landscaping the property. All will be beset with the problem of costs — which comes first — the new washing machine or the rose bed, shrubs or drapes. Obviously, there can only be one answer...for the first year or so the house must be furnished at the expense of the landscap-

ing. However, this doesn't mean that the garden has to be a wilderness or mud pile. Fortunately you can fill your garden with colour and fragrance with the outlay of only a few dollars. The answer is in a few packets of annual seeds which will quickly supply vivid splashes of gay colour. These too can be used to hide unsightly raw spots until the garden can be given a "lived-in" look.

Planning borders — The real beauty of any garden comes from the flower beds. These are usually created in the form of borders along the side and the back of the garden. In larger gardens they often form the dividing line between the back lawn and the vegetable garden.

Borders are usually classified into three main types, the annual, mixed and shrub borders.

In the annual borders are grown petunias, zinnias, marigolds, etc. *Annuals are plants which produce roots, stems, leaves, flowers and seeds all in the one season, then die.*

In the mixed border, as you might expect from the name, can be grown annuals, biennials, perennials, flowering bulbs and even shrubs and evergreens. By combining all these plants you can maintain a large and varied show of bloom from the time the first snowdrop or crocus bursts into bloom in the very early Spring until the last snapdragon or chrysanthemum falls prey to "Jack Frost" late in the Fall. Furthermore, the shrubs and the evergreens will lend character to the garden during the Winter season. The evergreens and shrubs always prove a tremendous attraction for the winter birds. In fact it's almost impossible to lure the birds to the garden without a fairly extensive evergreen and shrub planting.

In larger gardens there is usually room for a shrub border. Shrubs provide a garden with dignity. The flowers of some add beauty while others with symmetrical shaped foliage dress the garden with gracious form. Often shrub borders are planted to screen an unsightly view.

For young couples who have just moved into their first home, and with limited means, it is usually best to start with annual borders and then gradually change some of them over to the shrub or mixed border types. In the case of new subdivision homes the soil will need building up considerably before it is advisable to plant the more costly shrubs, evergreens and perennials. Annuals will give excellent colourful results the first season even if the soil is poor, by adding plenty of inexpensive humus and fertilizer. As a rule try to keep the edges of the borders straight, but if the garden is large, edges can be scalloped in long sweeping curves. Width is the all important factor in making any border. Don't be afraid of making borders wide. Most home gardeners make their flower borders far too narrow, and so do not have the room to hold the three groups of plants necessary to a successful flowering border.

For the annual border six feet is the minimum width, but eight feet is much better. Eight feet is the minimum width for the mixed or shrub border, and ten to twelve feet is the ideal width.

At the front of the bed you place the low growing plants which can vary from 4 to 15 inches in height. In the center of the border you plant those that grow from 15 to 24 inches high. At the back go the really tall growing plants.

If you have a narrow border which needs widening, or have no border at all, it is strongly recommended you get out pencil and paper and plan the border on paper first.

Preparation of the new border — Decide what type of border you ultimately want — annual or mixed — and work towards it. The first year can be annuals to which you gradually add perennials or shrubs. Having decided on the width, you'll have to know the length in order to calculate the area in square feet. If it is fifty feet long and eight feet wide, then the area is 400 square feet. This gives us the key to the amount of humus and fertilizer needed.

The humus is applied to moderately good garden soils at the rate of six bushels per hundred square feet. For the 400 square feet we would need 24 bushels. If the soil is heavy clay or very light sand 10 bushels per hundred square feet would be needed, or a total of 40. There are several types of humus which will do the job. Materials processed from sewage, peat moss, well rotted barnyard manure, discarded mushroom manure, or material from the home compost heap are excellent forms of humus.

Before working the humus into the soil scatter a complete fertilizer or plant food over the soil at the rate of 4 pounds per 100 square feet. For the 400 square feet of the mentioned new border we would need sixteen pounds. The best way of applying fertilizer is to put it into the same spreader we use for feeding lawns. Just set the dial on the spreader at the 4 pounds per hundred square feet rate to make sure the fertilizer is evenly distributed over the entire border.

Some people like to dig in the humus and fertilizer with a shovel, but it will be easier for you to hire a man who does custom rotary tilling. Twice over with one of these machines and its whirling tynes

Petunias and snapdragons are the backbone of the annual border.

will have thoroughly mixed together the fertilizer, humus and the top six to eight inches of soil. What's more the tilling leaves the soil in such a fine condition that it's possible to plant the annuals using only the hands. Since rotary tillers leave the soil in a rather puffed up condition it's advisable to rake it once before starting to plant.

Seeds or plants? — The experienced home gardener can grow a good many annuals from seed, but for the newcomer to gardening it is recommended that they buy plants from a reliable local grower. Your local nurseryman, garden club, or florist will be able to give you the names of growers who have a good reputation.

Buy good stock — Always buy short plants which are out of bloom. Of course late in the season this may not be possible. If you can find a plant grower who hardens off his plants before selling them to you, so much the better. By hardening them off we mean that he sets them out in the cold frame or hot bed and gradually accustoms them to the colder outside air each day by removing the sash for gradually lengthening periods. Such plants will take quickly

Midget Blue, the best dwarf variety of Ageratum, is planted at the front of the border.

to their new location in your garden.

When buying a lot of plants the cheapest way is to purchase those grown five or six dozen to a seedling flat. Do not make the mistake of buying overly large plants in bloom. All too often they have been kept in the greenhouse or hot bed until just before you bought them. This means that a lot of the vigour of the plant has been used up in producing the flowers. Invariably the growth will be soft and will suffer a set back when set out in the ground.

Planting annuals by size

Front of the border — The first row of plants is spaced six inches from the front of the border. For this row you will find a wide selection of free blooming flowers. If you like a real sky blue, then the clusters of the ageratum will delight you. "Midget Blue", the All-America Silver Medal winner is the best dwarf variety — these plants grow 2 to 3 inches high and are completely covered with small blue flowers.

It would be hard to find a more useful dwarf edging plant than sweet alyssum. You can create a fine show at the front of the border by alternating Royal Carpet, Carpet of Snow and Rosie O'Day, which is the first pink alyssum to keep its colour during the hot part of the summer. Royal Carpet is a truly dwarf alyssum in a rich violet blue, and Carpet of Snow will soon produce a fine mat of pure white flowers.

For sandy soils which become hot and dry in the Summer you can't go wrong with portulaca. Plants form dense mats a few inches high and are covered with flowers all season. The best variety is the all double mixture, as its colour range includes a wide variety of shades.

"Petite" strain marigolds, one of the All-America winners for 1958 take some beating for the front edge of the annual border. This new class of extra dwarf double French marigolds is distinctly different. It produces an abundance of very early flowers and has a very long blooming period. Plants are compact, about 6″ high with a spread of about 10″ and flowers in great profusion, often with 50 blooms per plant in full flower at one time. There are four varieties in this new class — Petite Gold, Petite Harmony, Petite Orange, and Petite Yellow.

Other excellent plants for edging are dwarf candytuft, lobellia, nierenbergia, verbena and dwarf celosia (cockscomb).

Middle of the border — The second row of flowers is spaced back 12 inches from the first. For soils that are really poor the dwarf double nasturtiums called the Gleam hybrids will make a fine showing. Whatever you do don't feed nasturtiums, otherwise they'll produce all leaves and very little flowers.

One of the most satisfactory dwarf flowers is the Tom Thumb zinnia. The plants grow eight inches high, are compact in habit and are covered with flowers of the Lilliput type. Another excellent annual for this position is the phlox·Drummondi. This annual resembles the perennial phlox in everything except height. Most varieties grow six to ten inches high, although the tall large flowered type will grow 12 to 15 inches in height. Glamour, the 1960 All-America winner, is one of the best annual varieties. It has large, showy wonderful glowing salmon coloured flowers. Plants grow about 12 to 15 inches high, are vigorous and free blooming. There is also a mixture of the same height which is listed in most seed catalogues as Tall Large Flowered.

To fill the center section of the border there is such a large number of flowers that it can be very confusing to the beginner. You can plant asters, celosia, annual gallardia, many varieties of marigolds, mignonette, nicotine, petunias, salpiglossis, tall stock and zinnias.

You could start off with a row of petunias, 15 inches back from the annual phlox or dwarf zinnias. In this row it would be hard to beat Coral Satin. The flowers are a rich coral red which gradually becomes salmon pink in very hot weather. The colour is bright but soft and blends well with many others. The plants are neat in habit and very free flowering.

A further 15 inches back you could plant White Satin petunias. This is a new addition to the Satin group of petunias having pure white blooms slightly crinkled at the petal edges. Finally, a further 15 inches back you wouldn't go wrong by planting a row of single asters. The large, single daisy-like flowers are very beautiful and are unsurpassed for their decorative effect. Colours range from the most brilliant to the daintiest pastel shades.

Back of the border — The last row is planted eighteen inches further back and this is where we use the tall growing annuals. Again the choice is a big one. It includes snapdragons, tall plumed celosia, cleome (spider plant), cosmos, annual hollyhock, larkspur, marigolds, salvia, scabiosa and zinnias.

For the beginner the tall growing zinnias, marigolds or snapdragons are the best choice. In zinnias, the giant dahlia flowered would be excellent for this purpose. They are outstanding both for the exquisite form of their long stemmed flowers, which resemble giant dahlias, and for the lovely shades in their colour range. They grow about 5 inches across and 2 inches or more in depth. The well branched sturdy plants grow 3 feet high. As far as marigolds are concerned, the Climax varieties are undoubtedly the best for planting at the back of the border. These are tall growing and giant flowered. The almost globular blooms grow up to 5 inches across and 3 inches deep. The sturdy plants grow 2 to 2½ feet tall and bear a tremendous number of flowers.

Royal Carpet Alyssum is one of the most useful edging plants for the front of the border.

Temporary hedge — In order to look its best any flower bed or border needs a suitable background. We usually provide this by planting a hedge along the back of the border. Unfortunately it takes three or four years for worthwhile hedge material to grow large enough to furnish an effective background.

Take a look through your seed catalogue and you'll be able to find some fast growing annuals which can be used for two or three years until the hedge has grown tall enough.

One of the best plants for this purpose is the spider plant or cleome. This tall growing sub-shrub is a hardy annual which originally came to our northern gardens from South America and bears white and purple blooms. Its maximum height varies from four to six feet. The beginner at gardening will like this flower because it can be easily grown from seed sown directly at the back of the border or elsewhere in the garden. It is probably best to get a jump on the season by starting the spider plants indoors like the rest of the annuals and then setting them out in the garden around the 24th of May. The time to sow the seed directly in the garden is around the first of May. In warmer parts of the continent seed could be planted a week or two earlier, while in the colder parts, sow a few days later.

Set the started plants two feet apart or thin the seedlings to the same distance when they reach two inches in height. Be sure to prepare the soil well by adding humus.

The spider plant, Cleome, makes a fine temporary hedge or accent plant at the head of the annual or mixed border.

Sowing & transplanting

Sowing seed outdoors — A finely pulverized seed bed is essential for good germination whether it be sown outdoors or in. Do not sow the seed when the soil it too wet. Trying to prepare wet soil will cause hard lumps to form when the soil dries out, and the tiny seeds will not have correct contact with the soil or be covered sufficiently.

Preparation of seed bed — Just as soon as the soil is workable in the Spring, dig it to a depth of 6 to 8 inches. At the same time work into the soil a quantity of humus at the rate of 6 bushels per hundred square feet and a complete fertilizer at the rate of 4 pounds per hundred square feet. Just before sowing time, finely pulverize the soil and make a smooth and level surface.

Seeds can either be broadcast or sprinkled in shallow rows. The latter method is the best for the beginner to gardening. Seeds are then covered lightly with fine soil. A good rule of thumb for covering the seed is to cover three times the width of the seed. The best ways to get fine soil is to run some good garden loam through a piece of fly screen, or you can buy one of the prepared top soil mixtures from your local garden store or center. The one prepared for african violets is excellent for this purpose. After covering, tamp the soil gently with a flat board so that there is close contact between the soil and the seed.

It's important not to let the soil dry out otherwise many of the seeds will not germinate. During this germinating period any watering that is done should be carried out most carefully. Use the finest spray of water possible.

Once the plants have reached 2 inches in height you can either thin them out to the necessary distance apart or you can transplant to other parts of the garden. In the case of zinnias, it is most important that the transplanting be done before they reach two inches in height.

Try a hedge with Burning Bush — For a temporary hedge in a sunny location you can't go wrong with planting kochia or burning bush, as it's popularly called. It's called the burning bush because all Summer long it's a beautiful shade of light green and closely resembles a neat, formal evergreen hedge and then in the Fall the entire plant takes on a rich deep red colour, very reminiscent of the burning bush mentioned in the Bible.

If you want to capture the children's interest you can even grow and shape it into a full size chesterfield and chairs. This could be so life-like that it would be extremely hard to tell it from real furniture.

The kochia is the neatest and showiest of the annual hedge plants. They grow 3 to 5 feet high, are shrub-like and have narrow leaves almost resembling evergreen needles.

Time to sow the seed indoors is during the first part of April, or outdoors in the first week of May. Thin or set the plants eighteen inches apart in a location where they'll get full sun. Keep a few plants in reserve in case any of those set out to form a hedge fail to grow satisfactorily.

Sowing seeds indoors — Not all kinds of flowers benefit by early planting indoors. Some are actually handicapped by this treatment because it involves transplanting. However, for certain types, mainly petunias, snapdragons, pinks, salvia and lobelias, this early start is the main factor in providing satisfactory performance in the garden.

For these early-planted flowers a good rule to follow is to sow the seed 8 weeks before you expect good growing weather in the garden. This allows the seed to get started and develop into husky plants for setting out. If you jump the gun and start too early the plants are apt to grow tall and spindly and so be hard to plant.

Two or three weeks later there are some other annuals which can be sown directly in the garden but which benefit from an early start too, and which transplant well. These include asters, marigolds, salvia and verbenas.

A sunny kitchen window is a good spot to start plants because the air in the kitchen is generally more humid than other parts of the house and water is always handy when the plants need a drink.

No elaborate equipment or special knowledge is needed to start seeds indoors. Any container which will hold soil to a depth of 2 to 3 inches will be satisfactory. A milk carton cut in half the long way is an ideal small unit and so is a flower pot in which Spring flowering bulbs are forced. Regular seed flats are larger in size but no more effective. Fish flats used to transport finnan haddie and other kinds of fish make ideal seedling flats.

You will also need the planting mixture itself, and a pane of glass to cover the containers. The glass is used to prevent the surface of the soil from drying out too quickly. Where no glass is handy, then a sheet of cellophane or even a sheet of newspaper will do the trick.

The planting mixture need not be extra fancy. One third sand and two thirds soil is usually satisfactory, although for fine seed like petunia, a layer of vermiculite is desirable at the very top. *Don't use fertilizer of any kind in your mixture.* Fill the container to within a half inch of the top, pressing the soil down firmly with a flat, smooth piece of board. Draw shallow rows 2 inches apart, figuring about three times the diameter of the seed as the right depth to plant. An exception is petunias which should be sown directly on the surface and not covered at all.

Sow the seed thinly in the furrows, cover lightly, press down gently with a flat piece of board. *Don't attempt to water the seed from the top,* but run an inch or so of water in the sink and let it soak up from the bottom. Any container should have one or more holes in the bottom to permit drainage, and this is a handy way to get water into the container without disturbing the surface. Just as soon as the surface of the soil begins to show moisture remove the container, cover with the pane of glass or piece of cellophane, followed by a newspaper. Then place it near a window where the temperature runs around 65 to 70° and be patient.

Usually you won't have to water again until the seeds have sprouted. Check frequently to see when sprouting occurs so that the glass cover can be removed to provide ventilation, prevent drawing up of the plants, and to prevent a fungus disease called "damping off". As the plants begin to reach 1 to 2 inches in height and start to crowd each other, transplant to other containers such as handy peat pots, small clay pots or veneer plant bands.

Pinch back the plants that grow tall and spindly, and when the weather is settled transplant to the garden, with the pride and satisfaction of growing your own plants!

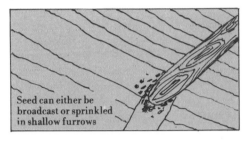

Seed can either be broadcast or sprinkled in shallow furrows

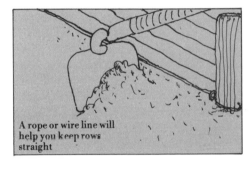

A rope or wire line will help you keep rows straight

To prepare the soil, dig in humus and fertilizer

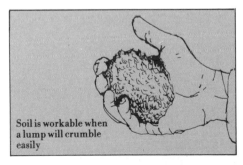

Soil is workable when a lump will crumble easily

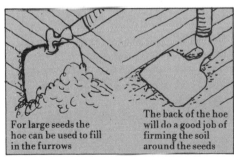

For large seeds the hoe can be used to fill in the furrows

The back of the hoe will do a good job of firming the soil around the seeds

A finely pulverized seed bed is essential for germination

Straight rows are best achieved by measuring the distance apart with a ruler

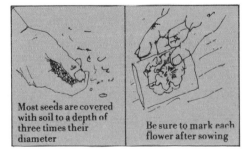

Most seeds are covered with soil to a depth of three times their diameter

Be sure to mark each flower after sowing

Annuals that need to be sown in the late Fall — The larkspur or annual delphinium and the single and double annual poppies are spectacular plants in any garden. These annuals always draw admiring glances and comments from almost everyone, yet very few are grown each year.

Why should this be so? The main reason for most home gardeners failing to plant them is the plants' inability to stand transplanting. This means that they cannot be treated like petunias, zinnias, marigolds and most of the other annuals. Normally these are sown indoors during either March or April and the plants are ready for setting out in the garden from the middle of May onwards.

On the other hand, larkspur and the annual poppies need to have their seed sown where they are to grow in the garden. The best time to do this is late in the Fall just before freeze-up time. Unfortunately, most people have lost interest in outdoor gardening by this time of the year and are very unwilling to face the chilly winds of November in order to sow some flower seeds.

This is a big mistake because the spectacular show of bloom in the garden the next Summer will more than make up for the few minutes work required.

Larkspur — Like its perennial cousin the delphinium, is a tall growing flower which is indispensable for planting at the back of the annual or mixed border. No flower, annual, biennial or perennial, makes a better cut flower. The graceful plants have a soft feathery foliage, and columns of double flowers in exciting tints of violet, blue, pink, red and pure white.

It's best to choose a location where they'll get full sun but you can get some fairly good results in partially shaded locations. To show their best these tall growing flowers need planting against the darker background of a hedge or wall. This also protects them from winds or heavy rains.

As mentioned before, the best time to plant larkspur is during the month of November. The seed will lie dormant until early next Spring when it will receive the ideal cool conditions for best germination. After the plants are one to two inches high you thin them so that they stand 8 to 10 inches apart.

The preparation of the soil for sowing is the same in the Fall as it would be in the Spring. Dig into the soil a quantity of humus at the rate of 5 or 6 bushels per 100 square feet. This means that you need a bushel of humus for an area 4 feet by 3 feet. Mix the soil and humus thoroughly together and then rake to level and to remove any stones, pieces of wood or other debris.

It's very easy to sow the seed. After pulverizing the soil well and mixing it thoroughly with the humus you rake it level and you're ready to sow. For each clump, scatter a few seeds over the surface of the soil and gently press them into the soil with a board. A good idea is to cover with no more than $\frac{1}{8}$ of an inch of vermiculite. This keeps the soil moist and helps you to easily recognize the seeded area. To make doubly sure you don't disturb the seeded area next Spring, mark the areas with small stakes.

The best kinds for the garden are sold as the Supreme or Steeplechase types depending upon where you buy the seed. Burpee Wonder is another excellent strain especially if you want to grow good cut flowers.

The best time to sow larkspur is in the late fall.

Another way of handling larkspur is to sow the seed in November in 3 inch clay pots, plant squares or peat pots. Place these in a coldframe over Winter and then transplant to the garden as soon as the soil is workable next Spring. Larkspur started this way will not receive a setback at transplanting time, and they'll be in the garden soon enough so that they'll develop the necessary size while the weather is still cool.

Poppies — The annual poppies are delightful for growing in any garden not only because of their brilliantly coloured blooms but because of the tremendous number of flowers produced by each plant. It's true that the individual blooms are rather short-lived but there are always new ones opening every day to take their place.

There's no doubt that the Shirley strain is the best to grow. Veterans of World War I were very familiar with the common red field poppy of Europe, so much so that John McRae immortalized it in his famous poem, "In Flanders Fields". The Shirley strain is a much improved form of this poppy and now only faintly resembles its well remembered ancestor. Single and double forms are available from most seedsmen. Sweet Briar is an exciting double kind whose deep rose-pink flowers will catch everyone's eye. You can also buy the All Double Mixed which is a collection of pinks, scarlets, whites with many of them delicately shaded with a second tint. American Legion produces orange-scarlet single flowers of enormous size and great beauty. This is the variety that closely resembles the Flanders poppy although it is greatly improved.

Best time to sow the seed is in November at the same time you sow larkspur. Don't make the soil too rich or you'll get all green growth and few flowers. A good way of handling the seed is to mix it with fine sand and spread this mixture thinly over the soil. Then barely cover with no more than $\frac{1}{8}$ of an inch of very fine soil. Use one of the commercially prepared soil mixes for this purpose or put some of your own soil through a piece of fly screen.

Poppies need full sunlight and a location towards the back of the mixed or annual border. Just as soon as the plants are about 2 inches high next Spring thin to 15 inches apart.

Annuals that flower well indoors — Dwarf marigolds and nasturtiums, two fugitives from the Summer garden, make excellent Winter flowering house plants if grown in a sunny window.

Children at home or in school can have a lot of fun sowing the seed and caring for the plants during the Winter months when outdoor activity is restricted. You will probably find that Fall and Winter interest in gardening is usually carried over into the Spring and Summer months.

Experience has shown that pots of dwarf marigolds bought when in bloom from the florist will give up to 2½ months of colourful bloom with quality equalling those grown outdoors. The main ingredients for producing such bloom is the day-to-day care of watering and pinching off the blooms as they fade.

Florists say that they have their best success with the variety Cupid which has large-sized, double yellow blooms that are extremely long lasting. Yellow Supreme is another good marigold for indoor flowering. It grows 30 inches tall in the garden but only to about 12 inches indoors.

The Petite strain of marigolds does well when grown indoors. They burst into flower quickly and they have a free-blooming habit.

As far as the nasturtiums are concerned dwarf double varieties are the best to grow. They form in a compact bush and produce delightfully scented flowers, which are borne on long stems.

For Winter flowering indoors the dwarf marigolds may be sown at any time from the 1st of November to the middle of February. Nasturtiums should not be sown until January or early February when the days start to lengthen and the sun becomes stronger.

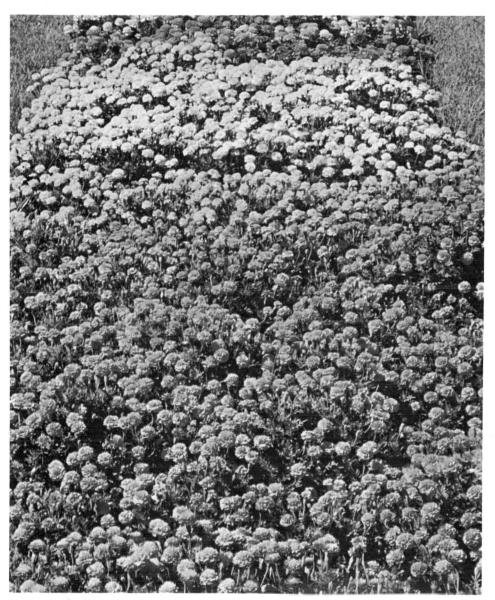

Petite marigolds are hard to beat for planting at the front of any flower bed.

There are two equally successful ways to grow them; use one of the new annual seed starters, or sow the seed yourself in pots or other containers. Many persons are using these new annual seed starters which consist of seed sown in vermiculite. All you have to do is water them and place them in a warm sunny window and in a very few days the seedling plants appear. After the plants reach 1½ to 2 inches in height, you transplant them to seedling flats or small clay pots. In sowing your own seeds the best and easiest way of obtaining a suitable soil combination is to buy one of the commercial mixtures. The one prepared for african violets is excellent for germinating the seeds and for growing the plants after germination. You don't require a rich soil for germination but it should

be loose in texture, drain readily, and yet be able to hold moisture. In making up your own mixture use: 2 parts good garden loam, 1 part humus and 1 part coarse sand. For humus you can use peat moss, leaf mold, materials processed from sewage or well rotted barnyard manure. These materials should be thoroughly mixed together and then put through a coarse screen with a ¼ inch mesh. This same soil mixture can be used for potting up the plants.

Place some of the prepared mixture in a seedling flat, 3 inch clay pot or bulb pan and press it well into the corners and around the sides. Fill with soil to the top of the container and level to the edges without hard packing. Next, firm the soil with a piece of board so that the surface of the soil

is approximately ½ inch below the edges of the pot or seedling flat.

Care should be taken not to sow the seeds too thickly. In covering the seeds with soil after sowing, a good rule of thumb is to apply enough soil so that they are just out of sight. For this purpose use a soil that has been put through a ⅛ inch mesh screen.

After the seeds are covered with soil give them a good watering with a very fine spray and cover with a piece of moistened burlap or newspaper. Until the seed germinates sunlight will not be necessary but the room temperature should be 68-70 degrees. Just as soon as the seedlings begin to germinate, move to your sunniest window or they'll tend to grow tall and spindly.

When seedlings are 2 inches high it's time to move them to 3 inch clay pots using the same soil mixture as mentioned before. Flowering will take place about 8 or 9 weeks after sowing the seed.

Nasturtiums will not stand transplanting so they should be sown in 3 inch clay pots, one seed to a pot. Plant ½ inch deep, cover and then water thoroughly. Place the pot in the sunniest window. The dwarf Gleam hybrids are the best variety for growing indoors.

Transplanting — In almost any flower garden there are occasions for a certain amount of transplanting, even if it is only to re-adjust the spacing between plants which have come up irregularly from seed sown directly in the garden.

The basic rules for moving plants are very simple. Disturb the roots as little as possible — use plenty of water.

To these ends it is desirable, if the soil is not already moist, to water your flower bed the day before you intend to do the transplanting. This gives the soil a chance to become thoroughly moist, not just muddy on the surface around the roots of the transplants. Similarly, a few hours before you move the plants from their flat, make sure they are well watered to encourage the soil to adhere to the roots and to hold together when you lift it with your trowel.

If the plants are to be moved from flats they will probably be growing about 2 inches apart. This is the ideal spacing because you can cut an adequate square of earth around each plant, lifting plant, roots and soil in one complete unit. The lucky plants moved this way hardly know it has happened, and go on developing without hesitation. Even better transplanting conditions result from the use of compressed peat pots which are fine for starting plants, and which are set directly in the ground, plant, pot and all in one unit. The roots then grow right through the walls of the pot and continue on into the garden soil.

If the ball of earth around the roots crumbles by accident during transplanting there is no need to despair, for even bare-rooted most plants will soon adjust to the new situation and take up growth again. In setting any plant in its permanent location it is important to make the hole deep enough so that the roots need not be curled or folded back in setting them in position.

Extremely long roots ought to be pruned rather than crumpled. Plants should be transplanted to the same level in the garden as in the flat or pot in which they were started.

Crackerjack is the first of the large flowered marigolds to bloom

Once in place, it is very important for you to firm the soil around the roots, eliminating air pockets and welding the soil to that surrounding the transplant. This you can do by the pressure of your fingers, and then by watering. Of the two, watering is the more important, for all the crevices are filled, the soil particles silted into position and the plant firmly situated in its new location by this action.

It is better to do your watering by pouring around the base of the plant, and sprinkling is acceptable if you watch closely to see that the small plants are not being beaten to the ground.

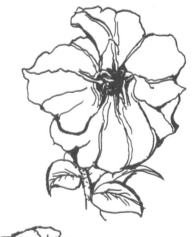

14

Zinnias add to the beauty of any garden

tablespoonful of complete plant food per gallon of soil.

This soil mixture should be fairly damp so that the soil will cling to the side of the plant bands. Fill with more soil to within a half inch of the top of the bands. This space is left for watering.

In addition to the hard-to-transplant flowers there are a growing number of home and commercial gardeners who are sowing seeds like snapdragons, nasturtiums, zinnias, etc., in this way and not doing anymore transplanting until they are set in the garden. The argument being that every time you transplant you disturb the roots and the plants receive a setback.

In each band or peat moss, plant two to five seeds according to their size. When the seedlings come up, then thin out to the strongest plants.

The seeds are covered to a depth about twice their diameter. After sowing give them a gentle soaking with water at room temperature and place the flat of plant bands in a sunny warm window, greenhouse or hotbed. Cover the flat with a sheet of glass and then a piece of newspaper or burlap until the first seed germinates.

As the season advances give more and more ventilation so that the plants will be well hardened off by planting time. When planting out time arrives prepare the soil as you would normally do. You will find that the thin wooden band will easily break away from the soil surrounding the plants and can then be gently set in the soil without disturbing the roots of the plant.

How to handle hard-to-transplant annuals — There are a number of flowers which object to being transplanted one, two or three times before being planted out in the garden. They don't like being sown in a seedling flat or pot, then transplanted when an inch or so high to another flat or pot and finally moved into the garden when outdoor planting time arrives. That means that if you want to get an early start with these flowers you must sow them in a container which will allow you to transplant them to the garden without disturbing the roots or the soil around them. As a matter of fact, unless you can treat a heavenly blue morning glory in this manner you won't get very much bloom before frost strikes in the Fall. Sown outdoors it is hardly worthwhile growing.

What can be done about it? The hard-to-transplant flowers can be started off indoors in thin wooden plant bands or peat moss. You can also use clay pots but you will find these expensive compared to the bands.

Wooden plant bands are set in a shallow box or seedling flat. Add an inch of soil and firm it down gently with the fingers. This soil mixture should be a little richer than that normally used for sowing seed because the seedlings are going to stay in these plant bands until they are moved outdoors. Even then the soil remains around the plants during their growing lifetime. Use a mixture consisting of three parts good garden loam, one part peat moss or material from the home compost heap and one part sharp sand. To this you add *one*

15

Easy to grow annuals

ASTERS — It's hard to beat asters for a good display in the garden and certainly for cutting there's no other annual to equal them. Unfortunately, over the past few years the aster wilt and the aster yellows have come along to plague us. Be sure to select wilt-resisting seed as seedsmen have been able to breed a certain degree of resistance to *wilt* in modern aster strains.

However, the disease called "yellows" remains the number one aster enemy. If your aster foliage turned yellow and the plants became stunted and died before flowering last year this disease was the cause of it.

Yellows cannot be cured after the plant has become diseased, but it can be prevented. The virus is carried exclusively by tiny leaf hoppers. You have to start dusting or spraying your asters with sprays or dusts as the seedlings appear and keep it up at weekly intervals during the Summer. This will prevent the infection of the plants. Because of this disease problem, *asters should not be planted in the same spot each year.* Select a new site each season.

Scarlet Beauty provides a sparkling cerise-scarlet colour. The larger American Beauty type flowers bloom from mid-season until frost. The 3 foot tall plants are wider at the bottom than the top and grow quite like a Christmas tree.

Early Giant is an exceptional class of early aster. They are the finest large flowered, wilt resistant asters yet developed. Plants start flowering early in August and the large California Giant type flowers are borne on strong heavy stems. Plants grow 1½ to 2 feet in height.

Try light blue, Peach Blossom and Rose Marie.

California Sunshine Improved Flowers have a beautiful, unique form. They're single with an attractive, quilled central disc. Plants measure 2½ to 3 feet high. Only mixed colours are available.

Super Giants are the largest of all asters. The most attractive large flowers are carried on top of long wiry stems. There's a wide colour range and flowers measure

Asters make a good display in the garden every year.

5 to 6 inches across. The plants are robust and reach anywhere from 2 to 3 feet in height. Flowering time is from late August until cut down by the frosts in late Fall.

Powderpuffs are a beautiful mixture of all the good aster colours. The plants have a neat upright habit of growth. Lovely pom-pom type flowers plus good straight stems makes them ideal for cutting. At present there are only mixed colours available. Plants grow 24 inches high and flower in August.

Single Rainbow Mixture. The large, single daisy-like flowers are very beautiful in their simplicity and are unsurpassed for decorative effect. Colours range from the most brilliant to the daintiest pastel shades. When located in good soil the plants grow 24 inches high. Flowering time is from

early Summer until frost. This strain is usually hardier than the double kinds.

PETUNIAS — Petunias are easily the most popular and widely grown annual garden flower in North America. They'll provide any part of the garden with a big and lasting splash of colour. Varieties in a wide colour range are available for planting in beds, borders, foundation plantings, rock gardens, window boxes, hanging baskets or containers around patios and outdoor living areas.

They'll grow well in both ordinary and fairly rich soil conditions. With plenty of moisture, they'll even give a good show of bloom when planted in poor soil. Petunias love the sun but they'll perform quite well in partially shady locations.

16

Coral Satin is the finest multiflora petunia.

About the only detrimental thing you could say about petunias is the fact that the seed is very fine, and because of this the beginner to gardening, or the average person, will find it hard to start their own plants. The best plan for most people is to buy started plants ready for setting out in the garden around the 24th of May. It's true that petunias will stand the effects of a light frost and so could be planted out in the garden around the middle of May or earlier. However, the plants won't really start to grow vigorously until the soil and temperature starts to warm up late in May and nothing is to be gained by rushing the season.

New hybrid varieties in all types have almost taken over from the older open pollinated types. They are more vigorous, free-flowering and the colours are more brilliant.

F.I. Hybrid All Double Petunias

This group of modern petunias is characterized by masses of brilliant coloured flowers carried on vigorous compact plants. The blooms are medium-sized, stiff-petalled and stand up well under adverse weather conditions.

Fl Grandiflora Petunias. These are large flowered, unusually fringed or slightly ruffled and produced on compact plants. Flowers are larger and slightly less free-flowering than the Multiflora hybrids.

One of the best of the Grandiflora hybrids is **Maytime**, a former All-America winner. It's the largest of this new group of extra large-flowered petunias and the flowers are coloured in exquisite salmon pink. Maytime stays in bloom for a long time. Often this flowering period lasts from early June until the first of November in the warmer parts of North America. Blooms average 3½ inches across. Perhaps their only fault is a tendency to fade out a little during extremely hot weather. Plants have a very compact base-branching habit with a spread of up to 2½ feet and grow 1 foot in height. Nice for window boxes, beds and borders.

Blue Lustre is considered to be the best of the deep purple blue petunias.

Marigolds like the Climax Toreador originated in the southwestern United States and Mexico.

MARIGOLDS — When Cortez conquered Mexico he found marigolds growing in the gardens there. In fact they're native to the southwestern United States and Mexico. Marigolds are the third most popular annual and are only exceeded in popularity by petunias and zinnias. With the development of newer and better varieties it may not be long before marigolds will be challenging the petunias and zinnias for their leadership.

Cortez took seed to Europe and they rapidly became the favourite flower for the devout to place at the altar of the Virgin Mary. This is how they got the name Mary's Gold, and then marigold. The large ones (Tagetes erecta) used to be called African marigolds, but today they're called American, which of course they are. The little ones (tagetes patula) are called French marigolds, although they also are natives of the North American continent and nowhere else in the world.

The marigold has much in its favour, it's easy to grow from seed and does well everywhere in North America, including Alaska and even Hawaii. Since they originated from the sunny, southwestern part of the United States and Mexico, marigolds like plenty of sunshine and will grow well under dry weather conditions. Marigolds and zinnias are the most easily grown from seed of all the annuals.

Climax Marigolds. These are undoubtedly the best tall growing giant flowered marigolds. Correctly grown, the almost globular blooms reach up to 5 inches across and 3 inches deep. They have almost the same quality as the indoor chrysanthemums. While of giant size, the fully double flowers have unusual grace and charm. The satiny petals are slightly ruffled and frilled and have a faint honey scent.

The sturdy plants grow 2 to 2½ feet tall and bear an abundance of flowers. All of them are large and carried on long, strong cutting stems from midsummer until frost.

Being hybrids, you'll get the best results if you plant Climax marigolds in soil that contains plenty of humus and fertilizer. To get the largest and best flowers it pays to disbud. Simply remove some of the flower buds while they are still small, so that those remaining will grow into flowers of much larger size. Time to disbud is just as soon as the buds are large enough to handle, usually when they reach the size of a bean.

Burpee's Red and Gold Hybrid are double hybrids of the American and French types. Flowers are exceedingly double, 2½ to 3 inches across, some are solid red while others are combinations of red and gold. The colour seems to vary with the season, at times it becomes almost pure golden yellow and at other times a bright, rich mahogany scarlet. The bushy upright plants grow 2 feet tall and flower in eight weeks from seed. They continue to bear profusely until the plants are killed by frost.

Spun Gold is the best of the early dwarf chrysanthemum flowered marigolds. Plants are bushy, erect and uniform in growth. They grow to a height of 12 inches and are covered with a mass of 2 to 3 inch double golden yellow flowers.

Cupid strain of marigolds is also very good for planting near the front of the annual or mixed border. They produce dwarf plants growing 10 inches high and bearing a profusion of large double chrysanthemum-like blooms from early June until the heavy frosts in the Fall. Cupid orange, golden, primrose or mixed are the varieties available.

Petite strain marigolds one of a delicate class of extra dwarf double French marigolds has achieved wide popularity since it was introduced. It not only starts to bloom early, but has a very long flowering period. Plants are compact and grow 6 inches high with a spread of about 10 inches. There will often be as many as 50 blooms per plant in full flower at the one time. There are four varieties: Petite Gold, Petite Harmony, Petite Orange, and Petite Yellow.

Signet marigolds (tagetes) are not nearly as widely grown as they should be. These delightful plants only grow 4 to 6 inches high, but the dainty fern like foliage is covered profusely with flowers growing anywhere from ½ inch to an inch in diameter. Gnome is golden orange, and Lulu is canary yellow.

Mammoth. Another spectacular tall growing group of marigolds is known as the mammoth mum or chrysanthemum flowered. These produce giant flowered chrysanthemum-like blooms 3½ inches or more across. In addition to making a wonderful display in the garden, they are a rich source of attractive cut flowers from mid-season until frost. Plants grow 3 feet tall. Colours are gold, orange, primrose and yellow.

Glitters is another fine tall-growing chrysanthemum flowered marigold. It was good enough to be an All-America winner when it was introduced. The flowers are large with nicely fringed outer petals and are a clear soft yellow in colour. Plants grow about 3 feet tall; they are bushy and erect with long stems for cutting.

Crackerjack grows 30 to 36 inches tall and is one of the first of the large flowered marigolds to bloom. The uniformly double flowers grow 4 to 6 inches across in a full range of marigold colours from primrose yellow to brilliant orange.

Harmony Hybrid is a very fine mixture of dwarf double marigolds. The neat, dwarf compact habit combined with the very early free flowering character of the plants make this mixture an attractive flower for any garden.

Naughty Marietta is a fine single French marigold with flowers of golden yellow and mahogany brown. Plants grow to a height of one foot and are free flowering.

SNAPDRAGONS — The most exciting snapdragons you can grow today are the Rocket snapdragons.

Six separate colours and a mixture of the same are now available.

Rocket snapdragons are the first hybrid snapdragons bred especially for long-day, mid-summer blooming. In the past those we grew in our gardens gave a fine initial display of bloom towards the end of June and on into early July and then faded away with the summer heat. Later in September in the warmer part of the country, they would perk up and provide some end-of-the-summer blooms.

They have hybrid vigour which means lush foliage and strong erect stems to support the large flower spikes in the long-day heat of midsummer. These spikes will grow 3 feet tall under good growing conditions. They branch at the base and throw out 10 or more long spikes of bloom at the same time. Once the first burst of bloom is over they should be cut back to within 5 to 6 inches of the ground. It won't be too long before another big crop of flowers comes along. You can even expect still a third crop in the early Fall.

"They're just like greenhouse snapdragons" is the comment of many people who see the Rockets flowering for the first time. It is exciting to see the tremendous spikes and large flowers produced by garden snapdragons. The flowers open right to the tips of the long spikes and last a long time in the garden or as cut flowers. Like other snapdragons, they stand quite heavy frosts.

These hybrid varieties come in six distinct colours: Red Rocket, Bronze Rocket, Golden Rocket, Orchid Rocket, White Rocket, Rose Rocket and a mixture of the same colours.

Dwarf snapdragons are very attractive and will be welcome in any garden. One of the best strains, Magic Carpet grows 4 to 6 inches high. It is a delightful variety particularly suitable for planting at the front of the border, foundation planting, or in pockets in the rock garden. The dwarf compact plants bear a profusion of miniature blooms in quite a good range of colours. This variety is sold only as a mixture and no separate colours are available.

Magic Half Dwarf, growing 20 inches

Rocket snapdragons flower well in hot weather.

high is the best type for bedding. Flowers are particularly large and the colours are excellent. They range from bright scarlet, fiery crimson and a very dark red to golden yellow and pure white. These are available in separate colours or as a mixture.

Planting — Snapdragons, like petunias, have a very small seed, about 220,000 to the ounce. It takes up to three weeks for the seed to germinate which means it should be sown early in February to have vigorous plants ready to set out in early May. You'll need to sow the seed indoors or in a hot bed, then transplant twice in order to have the plants ready for early planting. Unless you get them set out in the garden in early May, you won't be able to take advantage of the snapdragon's extremely long flowering season.

Starting snapdragons from seed is not the easiest job to do in gardening. For most people, it is usually better to buy started plants. In order to make sure you will be able to get the plants of your choice, it is recommended you contact your plant grower in January to get him to order the seed and start it about the middle of February.

ZINNIAS — Fifty years ago home gardeners would have laughed in derision if anyone dared to suggest that whole gardens could be planted with zinnias and nothing else. Yet, so rapid has been the development of the modern zinnia from a small-flowered, coarse and unattractive plant to the hundreds of varieties available today, that an all zinnia garden is now possible.

When dahlia-flowered zinnias were introduced in 1919 — the modern variety was on its way. Today it competes, at least equally, with the petunia for top popularity among the annuals.

The nice thing about zinnias is that you can hardly make enough mistakes or have enough bad weather or soil to keep them from blooming. But the difference between the flowers produced by a struggling plant and well-grown one is so great that it certainly does pay to know what to do to get the best this fine plant has to offer.

There are three golden rules to remember for the successful growing of zinnias.

One — Zinnias thrive in warm weather, so it is no kindness to plant them too early in the garden. If the seeds sprout during a warm spell the little seedlings that have to endure chilly nights and cold soil become

There are so many varieties of zinnia that an all zinnia garden is a possibility.

"hardened" or stunted in the process and are slow to recover even after the weather warms up. On the other hand, seeds planted when both soil and night air are reasonably warm sprout quickly and plants grow at full speed, rapidly passing earlier planted rows and making better all around crops in the long run.

Two — Zinnias object to transplanting —the seed should be sown where the plants are to remain. While it is possible to transplant small seedlings successfully they, too, go through a shock period and recover slowly, while undisturbed seedlings go ahead without check.

Three — Zinnias, like most annuals, enjoy full sun — not shade. Zinnias are heat resistant to an extreme, but are not immune to drought. So don't worry about hot weather, the plants will love it, but if the

soil becomes dry and the leaves look grey and wilted in the afternoon, give the earth a good soaking around the base of the plants and watch how they recover and put on new growth!

Zinnias make fine cut flowers. But there is a little trick here too. Cut the flowers in the later afternoon when the plants are in slightly wilted condition, plunging the stems in water at once. The foliage and petals are apt to look fairly limp at that time, but if you put the cut flowers in a cool place over night you'll be astonished to see how they have perked up by the morning, making arrangement easy.

Zinnias are best selected on the basis of their height: Tall types grow two and one half to three feet, dwarfs from six to 12 inches.

Giant Dahlia Flowered Zinnias are outstanding both for their exquisite form and their lovely colours. Well grown plants will reach three feet in height and produce great numbers of flowers five inches across and two inches or more in depth. These will provide the garden with masses of spectacular colour and, because of their keeping qualities and long stems, will prove excellent for cutting.

Giant of California strain produces the largest flowers, averaging five to six inches across. These have a very distinctive shape that is most graceful and desirable. They are flatter than dahlia-type zinnias and their overlapping petals are more loosely placed. The well branched plants grow vigorously and reach about three feet in height. Many long, strong stems are developed — each crowned with a beautiful flower about one inch in depth.

Cactus-Flowered Zinnias. Many home gardeners feel giant hybrid or cactus-flowered zinnias are the most exquisite so far. These include first and second generation hybrids which develop soft, airy flowers five inches or more in diameter and free from the traditional zinnia stiffness. The free-blooming plants are strong growers and reach two and one-half to three feet in height. All varieties are equally good for massing in the garden or for use as cut flowers.

Burpeeana Giant Zinnias. This is the first of a new type of zinnia which produces immense flowers up to six inches across on short, bushy, compact plants that only grow 2 feet high. The first flowers start appearing when the plants are about 15 inches tall. This medium tall habit makes the Burpeeana zinnia especially valuable for beds, borders and low foundation planting.

The huge flowers have quilled and ruffled petals in all the loveliest combinations of colours. The full colour range includes lively orange, glowing gold, soft yellow, luscious pink, rose and salmon shades, glistening white, vibrant red and soft violet.

Semi-Tall medium flowered varieties

Ortho Polka is one of the best kinds in this group. It's gaily striped, beautifully formed 4 inch flowers will be a welcome addition to any garden. Newer colour combinations are now strongly slanted towards the popular yellow and red, orange and red, and a good representation of rose and white.

Cut-and-come-again Zinnias. More of these delightful zinnias are planted each year. The fully double, well rounded flowers about 2½ inches across are freely produced on long stems ideal for cutting. The compact, branching plants grow 1½ feet tall under average conditions.

Lilliput Zinnias are confusing to some people. They think that the word Lilliput refers to the size of the plants, but actually refers to the small pom-pom like flowers. Plants grow 12 to 18 inches tall and are literally covered from early Summer until frost with double blooms one to 1½ inches across. The colour range covers all the traditional zinnia colours. Lilliput zinnias are especially suitable as an edging for the taller varieties.

Dwarf varieties

Tom Thumb is a lovely little zinnia with plants only 6 to 8 inches in height which bloom profusely from early Summer until late Fall. Excellent for borders, edging, or for growing as pot plants. There is a good colour range.

Zinnia Linearis is also worth growing, especially if you like to arrange flowers. Plants grow 12 inches high and are covered with deep one and one half inch, orange-yellow blooms that have a deeper stripe down the center. This variety is an early bloomer and its leaves are also attractive.

Little Cupid zinnias are very delightful, compact plants about a foot high and bear small double flowers rarely exceeding an inch in diameter. Colours are orange, scarlet, pure white and yellow.

Snowtime is a good white cactus flowered zinnia.

Tom Thumb zinnias, a dwarf variety, come in a good color range.

Sweet peas are beautiful sweet-scented flowers.

SWEET PEAS — This lovely annual, which can attain 6 feet in height and bear beautiful sweet-scented flowers, is the envy of many home gardeners. While some may find difficulty in growing them successfully, good results should follow if you note their particular likes and dislikes.

When selecting seed bear in mind that the heat in July and August is a real killer for sweet peas. Aim to purchase the heat resistant varieties now on the market. You could buy several of these and see which does the best in your garden.

Floribunda sweet peas is a new strain developed from the famous Cuthbertson varieties. This variety has heat resistance, long stems, tall vigorous vines, plus the new multibloom characteristic. If you grow them under good conditions you should get 5 or more large, waved and fragrant flowers per stem.

The early flowering Spencers are another variety that helps to beat the heat. These sweet peas flower 2 weeks earlier than the standard Spencers and should be in full flower long before the hot Summer weather arrives. The vines are less branching but the flowers are equally large, beautifully waved and long stemmed.

Sweet peas require a deep rich soil with good drainage — avoid like the plague sandy and acid soils, shady locations. Dig a trench 15 inches deep and wide, remove the soil and replace it with a prepared mixture. Use either a commercial type (that for african violets will do) or you can make your own. This should consist of 2 parts top soil to one part humus. To this add a complete fertilizer or plant food at the rate of 5 pounds per each foot of trench. Make sure you thoroughly mix the soil, humus and fertilizer before replacing in the trench.

Like the peas of the vegetable garden, sweet peas are legumes and it will pay to innoculate them with legume-aid. This preparation, in the form of a black powder, will ensure a better stand and encourage strong growth. It can be used on garden peas, lupins and beans as well — a 15 cent packet will innoculate up to 5 pounds of seed. Soak your seed in water overnight before planting. Just before sowing drain off the water and sprinkle the seed with the black powder.

As soon as the ground can be worked in the Spring plant the seed an inch or two apart in furrows 3 to 4 inches deep, covering lightly with not more than 1½ to 2 inches of soil. When the seedlings appear, gradually fill the furrow, water gently but thoroughly, making sure the water penetrates to the roots. Later, thin out to 8-10 inches apart.

You could try to beat the season by starting the seed indoors. Use plant squares (2 inch size) filled with a soil rich in humus. Sow the seed $\frac{1}{2}$ inch deep and place 3 seeds in each hole, then thin by replanting the strongest seedling when about an inch high. Seed sown indoors about the 10th of March will be ready for setting out in the garden towards the end of April.

When the young plants are $1\frac{1}{2}$ inches high place in position the support to hold the future plant erect. For this, birch bush is recommended — don't forget to secure it against high winds.

Once the plants commence blooming, keep picking the flowers — if you allow pods to form the vines will die.

Sweet peas have very long roots. Remember this when watering as the water must penetrate to about 10 inches deep in the soil. This is even more important during the hot summer months.

IMPATIENS — Is also known as the patience plant. It's a very useful plant for growing in the garden because it's one of the few flowers that will grow well in partly shady conditions. Flowers are quite large and single. Colours are red, white, pink or salmon. Very good for planting in window boxes, as a bedding plant, or in containers around patios or outdoor living area. The impatiens plant is a vigorous grower and needs setting 24 inches apart either out in the garden or in a window box.

BALSAMS — Balsams are old favourite flowers for beds and borders which have lost a little of their popularity. This is a shame, because the flowers are not only beautiful, but they are distinctive and add something a little different to the garden. They need a location where they'll get full sun and where the soil is rich and well drained.

Impatiens grow well in the shade

Balsams are excellent for planting near the front of the border.

The free blooming Glamour annual phlox has large showy flowerettes.

Dwarf nasturtiums are very popular and can also be easily flowered indoors.

ANNUAL PHLOX (Drummondi) —

Most home gardeners have at least two or three plantings of perennial phlox in their garden, but not too many use the annual phlox. Here is a flower that should be in everyone's garden.

This decorative annual jumps into bloom almost immediately after setting out in the garden. It stays in bloom the rest of the gardening season. Especially if you keep picking off the flower heads as they fade. You will be particularly fond of the endless variety of colours which range from crimson, lavender and purple, through pink, rose and buff to white. In a great many of these colours you get an eye of a different colour in much the same manner as with the perennial varieties. There are kinds that grow only 6 to 7 inches in height, while others grow 15 inches.

Annual phlox need planting in full sunshine. The type of soil doesn't matter so long as it's well drained. You will like this annual because it grows well even though the weather is dry. For early bloom it is best to buy some started plants ready for setting out around the 24th of May.

When planting seed yourself, either indoors or outdoors, don't expect the seed to germinate overnight, it usually takes around two weeks.

NASTURTIUMS are the flower if your soil is poor —

One of the problems in interesting children in gardening is the fact that so many of the flower seeds are much too small for their inexperienced hands to handle successfully. Children don't show much interest in learning to work with growing things unless they can do most of the actual job of planting the seeds and caring for the plants themselves.

An attractive flower with seeds large enough for even small children to sow is the old favourite — the nasturtium.

In the musical world a song which survives many seasons becomes a "standard". In the flower garden, nasturtiums certainly fit this description. Although no significant changes have occurred in this flower class for 20 years, it continues to be the fourth most popular flower grown from seed (after zinnia, marigold and petunia).

The reasons for this steady position in the gardener's favour are the same ones that make zinnias, marigolds and petunias popular. The plants are easy to grow and *they produce lots of flowers provided they are grown in poor soils.* Nasturtiums can be depended to grow and flower under whatever growing conditions are found in the garden.

Nasturtiums will produce more flowers and better results if the soil is not too rich, thus it is a good plant to locate where the ground is poorest and where you didn't get around to digging in any fertilizer. Too much fertility simply encourages heavy leaf growth which buries any flowers that might develop.

Nasturtiums don't transplant too well so the best thing to do is to sow the seed where you want the plants to bloom about the last week in April or later depending upon where you live. Make the holes three quarters of an inch deep and three inches apart. When the plants come through the ground you thin the dwarf varieties to nine or ten inches apart and the tall ones to eleven or twelve inches.

You can choose from a wide selection of delightful shapes and colour combinations. There are single or double flowers, tall, semi-tall or dwarf growing. Their varied colours, different shapes and refreshing fragrance make them wonderful for cutting. If you have some fair sized clumps of the nasturtiums planted around your garden you should be able to pick a bowlful of blooms every day from early June until frost comes. Nasturtiums have been known to bloom on the Gulf Islands off the Southeast coast of Vancouver Island on Christmas Day.

There are four major classes of nasturtiums from which to choose. Let's suppose you have a bank, rocky area, or strip of wasteland on the "other side of the fence", you might appreciate the rapid and spreading character of Tall Mixed Nasturtiums. This type make a rapid and very satisfactory ground cover, at the same time producing plenty of coloured single flowers. The same flower form is also available in Dwarf Single Mixed, but the plants don't cover so much area.

Then there are two types with semi-double or double flowers. One series has the word "gleam", in the variety name. These produce husky spreading plants two feet or more across. Then there is the series with the word "globe", or "gem" in the name. These are dwarf nasturtiums and can best be described as small forms of the Gleam Nasturtiums. You'll find the plants neat and compact, growing 10 to 12 inches in height, and so are excellent for edging, pockets in the rock garden, or the window box.

Cosmos makes a wonderful annual for planting towards the back of the border.

The dwarf double varieties are particularly fine. These plants grow in a compact bush form, reaching one foot in height and one and a half feet in diameter. The delightfully scented flowers are borne on long stems which makes them especially good for cutting. You can plant them in beds and borders, as edgings, in pockets in the rock garden and even grow them in pots on the patio. When danger of frost arrives in the Fall you can pot up some of these dwarf plants and they'll continue to give good blooms as house plants.

There is really only one insect pest that will cause nasturtiums any trouble and that is the *aphid*. If you notice black aphids attacking your plants, spray or dust them with insecticides.

COSMOS — Zinnias, petunias, and marigolds get far too much publicity and this means that the average home gardener doesn't plant some of the lesser known but still very delightful annuals such as cosmos, cynoglossum and balsam. You could improve the charm and delightfulness of your garden by planting clumps of them around the various beds and borders.

Anytime you have a few minutes to spare this week get out your seed catalogues and turn to the cosmos section. You'll soon see that this favourite of a few years ago has been all dressed up in new clothes by our plant breeders. During the past few years the cosmos has not been nearly so popular as it was 25 and 30 years ago. However, it is predicted that the newer varieties now available are going to change all this.

25

Cosmos provides beautiful Summer and Fall flowering plants which are not only decorative in the garden but also make excellent cut flowers. All varieties of cosmos are easy to grow and they'll thrive even in the extra light sandy soils. They prefer full sunshine but will perform reasonably well in partial shade.

CHINESE FORGET-ME-NOTS

One of the real joys of the Summer garden can be the delightful sky-blue flowers of the Chinese forget-me-nots or cynoglossum. In most seed catalogues you'll usually find the latter term used. Most of us have a soft spot in our heart for the springtime forget-me-not whose sky-blue flowers are a welcome and pleasant part of many a North American garden. Unfortunately, this lovely flower is a biennial which means that once it's finished flowering in the Spring the plants die.

This is where the cynoglossum comes into its own. Graceful loose sprays of large, forget-me-not type flowers are freely produced throughout the Summer on strong plants. They will stand the hottest Summer with ease. Plants grow 15 to 18 inches tall so they'll need planting 12 to 15 inches in from the front of the annual border or foundation planting.

Chinese forget-me-nots or cynoglossum have delightful blue flowers.

GLORIOSA DOUBLE DAISIES

Once in a while, a flower breeder creates something entirely different. The late Dr.

The Gloriosa double daisy is an exciting and colorful annual.

A. F. Blakeslee of the Carnegie Institution of Washington, D.C., started selecting and hybridizing our wild black-eyed Susans (rudbeckia) over 40 years ago. All this patient effort and care has resulted in the new gloriosa double daisy.

This perennial can be treated equally as well as a very exciting and colourful annual, flowering freely the first year from seed.

Gloriosa double daisy has rich golden yellow blossoms, some so fully double as to look like golden balls, others looser petalled with a contrasting dark velvet center to show on fully opened flowers.

Gloriosa daisy is just as easy to grow as the old black-eyed susans. Plants are upright in growth with luxurious green foliage. Long stemmed flowers are well supported above the foliage and measure 4 inches or more across. Under good growing conditions the blooms may reach 7 inches in diameter. All of the flowers open fully double and remain so, but it's only fair to say that some flowers will eventually open wide to display the contrasting black-button eye in the center. Double or semi-double, all the flowers will be admired.

Flowering begins when the plants are

about 2 feet high and continues while the bushy plants grow to over 3 feet. Start the seeds indoors about the 1st of March or even earlier. Just as soon as the soil is workable in the Spring you can set the plants out in beds, borders, foundation plantings or along fences.

JEWELS OF OPAR — Looking for something different for your garden? Try Jewels of Opar (talinum paniculatum). This lovely flower is not new to gardening but it's not generally available.

It is easily grown, can be sown where it is to bloom or started indoors and transplanted to its permanent location in the same way as petunias and other annuals. The seed germinates readily, the plants grow thriftily, withstand Summer heat and become more beautiful with each passing week.

Foliage is a bright, deep waxy green, growing about a foot high and forming a delightful setting for the air panicled stems which rise another 1½ feet above the foliage. Great multitudes of small cameo pink flowers are produced. The flowers open in the early afternoon and are so numerous they have an ethereal quality.

It seems as if you are looking into a pink haze when looking through the top of the plant. Next morning the flowers are all closed but each tip of the many branch stems has a ruby coloured seed ball so that the effect in the morning is entirely different although no less beautiful.

These stems make delightful fillers for cut flower arrangements where buds will open into new flowers each afternoon for a week or more. They are also nice to dry for winter bouquets.

SALVIA — Salvia or Scarlet Sage is one of the most brilliant bedding plants. It blooms from early Summer until frost. Very popular for bed, borders, edgings and for pot culture. Not many people realize that it can also be used for cutting. There

are tall and dwarf varieties. The seed must be started early indoors so as to have plants large enough to set out in the garden when the weather and the soil have become thoroughly warm.

SALPIGLOSSIS — A most colourful annual. Painted tongue, velvet trumpet, and salpiglossis are the names given to this very colourful but not very widely grown annual which comes to our gardens from Chile. It's unfortunate that it's not grown more frequently because the salpiglossis is just as spectacular and colourful in the garden as the gloxinia indoors. The flowers of the salpiglossis have the same rich Oriental colours as the gloxinia and the colour range is wider. You will enjoy the

beauty of this plant, particularly the way lavender-blues are netted with silver or dark blue and crimsons with gold.

The trumpet-shaped flowers somewhat resemble petunias in form and shape but are much larger.

The salpiglossis makes an excellent middle of the border flower. Dwarf strains grow 18 inches high whereas Bolero and Emperor grow 30 inches in height when planted in good soil. The blooms make long lasting, graceful and thoroughly delightful cut flowers.

Seeds should be sown indoors in March or outdoors during the last week in April. Seed sown indoors during March will produce flowering plants in early July. They will continue to bloom until the hard frosts

Salvia provides a brilliant show.

Salpiglossis provides the garden with Persian carpet colors.

27

of early Fall. Plants from outdoor seed won't be in flower until early August. The seeds are very small. Barely cover the seed with fine soil, well pressed down. Early sown plants must be kept growing without setback until time to move them to the garden around the middle of May.

Strains of salpiglossis need a sunny location in the garden with a rich sandy loam which contains plenty of humus. Before planting, dig into the soil a quantity of humus at the rate of 5 or 6 bushels per hundred square feet of bed area. For poor soils increase the amount of humus to 8-10 bushels per 100 square feet.

At the same time work into the soil a complete fertilizer at the rate of 4 pounds per hundred square feet. A complete fertilizer is one that contains balanced amounts of nitrogen, phosphorus and potash. These are the main essentials necessary for plant growth.

It's doubtful whether you will be able to find salpiglossis plants for sale at many garden centers this Spring when annual planting time arrives. If you're not able to grow your own plants, buy the seed and take it to your local plant grower and get him to start the plants for you. They're better grown in individual peat pots, veneer plant bands or clay pots rather than in seedling flats or the usual trays containing a dozen plants.

Commercial greenhouse flower growers should also take a second look at the salpiglossis for it makes an excellent greenhouse annual. In these days when the market is flooded with too many chrysanthemums the blooms of the salpiglossis can help to vary the cut flower diet. Seed should be sown around the end of September for bloom at this time of year.

VERBENA — This brilliantly coloured annual is one of the most under-rated. It is a most decorative plant, ideal for edgings, beds, ground cover, rock gardens, window boxes and for cutting. Flowers are borne in large trusses from midsummer until late Fall. Plants thrive in any well-drained soil and withstand drought well.

Giant verbenas product robust plants, 8 to 12 inches high and spreading 2½ feet and more across. The large blooms measure up to 1½ inches in width and appear very early in the season.

Dwarf Compact are fine for edging and pot culture. Instead of the plants being of spreading habit, these are of compact,

Verbenas are most decorative plants ideal for edging.

dense growth and are covered with beautiful blooms all through Summer until late in the Fall. The plants grow 6 inches high and 10 to 12 inches across.

Sow indoors in flats placed in a sunny location in time to be set outdoors in May. Seed sown in the open in May should bloom in mid-summer.

TITHONIA or MEXICAN SUNFLOWER — One of the most improved annuals in the seed catalogue is the Tithonia or Mexican Sunflower. The older varieties tended to grow very tall and occasionally you would find one peering into an upstairs bedroom window. Fortunately Torch grows 4 feet tall. It's perfect for adding accent and colour to the rear of the annual or mixed border.

The foliage is curiously cut or lobed and is a rich dark green in colour. Late in July it throws a profusion of dazzling red-orange flowers resembling handsome single dahlias. They grow 3 inches in diameter with broad, flat petals surrounding a fiery sun in the center.

Tithonias are used wherever tall backgrounds are needed. They make an excellent temporary screen and are especially good for cutting, so much so that they are worth planting just for the cut flowers.

Plant the seeds indoors during the first two weeks in April in individual small pots or veneer plant bands. Set out in the garden in full sun when the danger of frost is past.

28

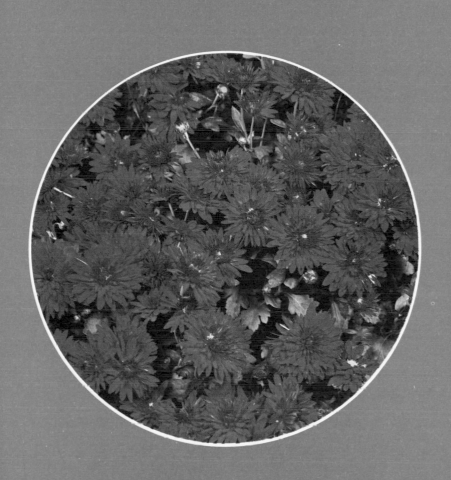

PERENNIALS

PERENNIALS

Chrysanthemums must be divided each year in the Spring

All about perennials

A perennial is a plant having roots which live more than two years. Year after year the root sends up new branches and flower stems which die when Winter approaches.

As their name implies, perennials add permanence to the garden and consequently have many uses. Each year when the weather turns warm you can be confident the roots will be spreading through the ground and later the plants will burst into brilliant displays of delightful flowers, adding grace to the garden for two or three weeks—a month or for several months.

Perennials are the backbone of the mixed border, are useful for planting among evergreens and shrubs in the foundation planting, pockets in the rock garden or the cutting garden.

Transplanting and Dividing

New perennials are produced by sowing seed, taking cuttings or dividing. Quite a number of perennials such as delphiniums, gaillardia, aquilegia and many others are mainly grown from seed, although a par-ticularly good variety of color in delphiniums can be propagated by divisions or even cuttings.

Iris, peonies and chrysanthemums are divided to obtain fresh vigor or to increase the number of plants. However the Korean chrysanthemums can be easily grown from seed sown indoors around the 1st of March. They will develop big clumps by fall and provide the garden with quantities of bloom. From then on choice colors can be divided each spring to obtain a supply of plants.

Single shasta daisies can be grown from seed or divided. The method you choose will be the one that is easiest for you. Double shasta daisies like Wirral Supreme must be propagated by cuttings or divisions.

When is the best time to transplant and divide perennials? There can be no one answer to this question. The best rule to follow is to divide or transplant anytime the plants start to lose vigor or when the quality and amount of bloom decreases. In the case of chrysanthemums this is done every May. Delphiniums are usually divided or replaced with new plants grown from seed every third year. Peonies can be left for ten years or longer in the same spot without dividing. Shasta daisies and phlox are best divided every third year.

Late summer and fall flowering perennials like chrysanthemums and asters are divided in the Spring while the spring flowering kinds such as Carpet Phlox and Aubretia can be divided either right after they've finished flowering in the spring or in August.

Propagation by cuttings is not a job for the average person or the beginner to gardening. Sowing seed or dividing the existing roots in the best plan and can be easily accomplished. In doing this be sure that the roots are dug most carefully to protect them from injury. Almost invariably the most healthy and vigorous shoots for division are those clustered around the outside of each clump. The center is usually the worn out part and is discarded. Each clump should contain a minimum of 3 or 4 shoots and the cut should be made with a sharp knife.

Most perennials are very hardy and are unharmed by the cold winters. Why do we have to provide winter protection? This keeps the perennials in cold storage by preventing alternate thawing and freezing of the soil during the winter and early spring. Perennials such as Russel Lupins which have long tap roots can be heaved partially or wholly right out of the ground and then killed by the alternate thawing and freezing of the earth.

That is why it is a good rule to give all perennials some winter protection. Plants that are set out in the garden must have protection to survive the first winter. Hay, straw, or cornsilk stalks make a good mulch. This should be applied two or three inches deep to be really effective. Do not use leaves as they become soggy and tend to smother the plants. Remove the mulch early in the spring just as soon as new growth appears.

Chrysanthemums provide Fall beauty in the garden

Mixed borders

In recent years the name "perennial border" has gradually been dropped and in its place we now have the term "mixed border". This has come about because we fill our perennial borders with a variety of plants, including annuals, perennials, biennials, Spring, Summer and Fall-flowering bulbs, and even some dwarf flowering shrubs. In this way we are able to create a maximum show of bloom during the entire growing season from early Spring until the frosts of autumn.

This being the case, you may want to make numerous changes in your border this Spring and during several Springs to come. Your past experience has probably been to have had a big display of bloom during April, May and June followed by disappointment for the rest of the season. Possibly too, you realise now your border was much too small to hold the three groups of plants which are essential to any border, be it annual, perennial or mixed. With a suitable background, such as a hedge or a fence, there should be a low-growing

group of plants at the front, a medium-height group in the center and a tall-growing group at the back.

A border with lawn or walks on all sides would have the tall-growing group in the center with the medium and low-growing plants located so there is a gradual drop from the center to the outer edges of the bed.

For those just starting a new border or re-designing an old one, the most important considerations are width, background and correct preparation of the soil. Most borders are far too narrow to accommodate the three groups of plants mentioned earlier. Six feet wide would be an absolute minimum with eight to ten feet being ideal. Flowers won't grow well if they are crowded, yet the tendency is to try to add just one more type of plant in an already overcrowded border.

Borders are usually located down the sides or across the back of the garden. This helps to surround it with an attractive flower frame. A hedge makes a suitable back-

ground since it is usually green and will grow as high or higher than any plants in the border. It's important to choose a true hedge plant as a background. It should be one with fibrous roots which stay close to the plant and do not reach out in the border to rob the surrounding plants as does the Chinese elm. In places like Chicago and Detroit and further south, the privet makes an excellent hedge. For the colder areas, the High Bush Cranberry is most suitable. Check with your local nurseryman about other suitable hedge plants.

A painted wooden fence also makes a good background for any border. Once erected and painted there is usually far less maintenance required than for a living hedge. Whichever you choose, be sure there is plenty of maintenance room between the hedge or fence and the plant material. In the case of the hedge it will need to be pruned and cultivated more than once each year. Wooden fences will need painting and repairing from time to time. In allowing room, remember to take into account the maximum growth of any plant or shrub.

In reorganizing your border you can change one-third of it at a time if necessary. This year you could replant the front part, the low-growing plants and flowers. Whether you follow this plan to replant and widen the whole border, or make a new one, it's important also to rebuild the soil. This doesn't mean replacing the soil unless it is completely useless.

Whatever the state of your soil, either sandy or heavy, the preparation is the same. Dig or till into the soil a quantity of both humus and fertilizer. The humus can be any one of the following: materials processed from sewage, peat moss, material from the home compost heap, well rotted barnyard manure, discarded mushroom manure, or leaf mold. Apply any of this humus at the rate of six to eight bushels per 100 square feet. The humus will open up the heavier soils, permit oxygen to reach the roots and materially improve drainage. In lighter soils humus

retains moisture thus preventing the water and fertilizer from seeping away quickly. Do this as soon as the soil is workable in the Spring. If the border is not too extensive the humus and fertilizer can be dug in by hand. The fertilizer you use should be a complete one containing balanced amounts of nitrogen, phosphorous and potash. Apply it at the rate of four pounds per hundred square feet.

At the front of the border you would plant perennials, annuals and one or two of the biennials. The following perennials are ideal for this location. Alyssum, arabis, armeria, alpine aster, aubretia, companula, carpatica, dianthus and carpet phlox (subulata), Of the annuals you could use annual phlox, portulaca, verbena, dwarf salvia, pinks, cockscomb, Tom Thumb zinnias, and petunias.

In the middle part of the border, you could plant aquilegias, hardy chrysanthemums, coreopsis, gypsophilia, bearded Iris, veronica and a host of other perennials.

You have a very wide choice of annuals suitable for planting in the center section of the mixed border. Asters, tall growing stock, gloriosa daisies, and many others.

Perennials planted at the back of the border would include: anchusa, hardy Fall-flowering asters, delphiniums, yucca, etc.

Tall flowering zinnias, snapdragons and marigolds are the annuals for the back of the border.

The various Spring, Summer and Fall flowering bulbs can be scattered in blocks down the front and middle of your mixed border. Don't forget to mark the bulbs with stakes, this will stop you interfering with them during Summer and Fall cultivation and planting when the leaves have ripened and died away. The dainty white snow-drops and the more spectacular blooms of the crocus will be the first flowers to bloom each Spring.

Mixed in with the early flowering bulbs can be the violas and pansies. These free-flowering plants will be in continuous bloom, provided they are regularly picked, until the really hot weather arrives. Then, if cut right back and fertilized again, they will give the front of the border renewed bloom during the late Summer and Fall.

Rock gardens filled with perennials can be very attractive

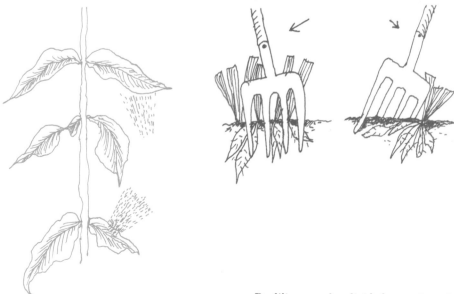

Spray both the top and undersides of the leaves.

Daylilies can be divided any time during the growing season, but the best time is after they have finished flowering.

Border planning

Tall — planted at the back of the border

Name of Plant	Height in Feet	Flowering Season	Colour of Flowers
Anchusa (Italica)	4	June-July	Deep sky blue
Asters (Hardy Fall Flowering)	2½-4	Aug.-Sept.	Pinks, violet, red mauve
Delphinium (Pacific Hybrid)	3-5	June-Oct.	Shades of blue, white and pink
Digitalis (Fox-glove)	3	June-July	Rose, white, yellow
Eremus (Giant Desert Candle)	4-8	July	Pink and Yellow
Helenium	2-3	June	Yellow and bushy
Hollyhocks (double & single)	4-6	June-Oct.	Separate colors of pink, salmon red, white, yellow and crimson
Iris (Japanese Iris)	2½-3	July	Blue, white, yellow
Lilies (various varieties)	3-6	June-Oct.	Many colors
Lythrum	2-3	July-Aug.	Purplish red
Pentstemon	3-4	July-Aug.	Coral red
Rudbeckia	4	July-Frost	Orange yellow
Yucca	4-6	June-July	Creamy white

Medium — planted in the middle of the border

Name of Plant	Height in Feet	Flowering Season	Colour of Flowers
Aquilegias (Columbine)	2-2½	May-June	Pink, blue, red, yellow, white
Chrysanthemums (Hardy)	2-3	Aug.-Nov.	Many colors
Coreopsis (Grandiflora)	1½-2	June-Aug.	Yellow
Gaillardia (Grandiflora)	1½-2½	June-Sept.	Yellow, red and orange shades
Gypsophila (Baby's Breath)	2-3	July-Sept.	White and pink
Iris (Bearded)	1½-3	May-June	Variety of colors
Lupines (Russel)	2	June-July	Various colors
Lychnis (Chalcedonica)	2-2½	June-Aug.	Scarlet
Poppy (Oriental)	2-3	June-July	Scarlet and salmon
Peonies	2-3	May-June	Red, white and pink
Phlox (Perennial)	2-3	July-Aug.	Many colors
Platycodon (Monks Hood)	2½	July-Sept.	Blue, white
Pyrethrum (Painted Daisy)	2-3	May-June	Rose red, white and pink
Veronica (Longifolia)	2-3	July-Sept.	Violet blue

Dwarf — for front of the border

Name of Plant	Height in Feet	Flowering Season	Colour of Flowers
Alyssum (Saxatile Compactum)	12 in.	April-May	Yellow
Arabis Alpina	6 in.	April-May	White and pink
Armeria (Sea Pink)	12 in.	May-Aug.	Pink shades
Aster Alpinus	9 in.	May-June	Blue
Aubrietia	4 in.	April-May	Purple, red and pink
Campanula Carpatica	6 in.	June-Oct.	Blue-white
Dianthus (Perennial Pinks)	12-18 in.	May-June	Variety of colors
Phlox Subulata (carpet)	4-6 in.	April-May	Pink, white, blue, mauve and wine red

The most popular perennials

Perennials make a fine display in the Spring garden

Anthemus or Golden Daisy

Achillea or Yarrow

ALYSSUM—(cloth of gold)—This is one of the most popular, and easiest to grow of the hardy perennials. It's a very free bloomer, starting to flower in April, and continuing until some time in June. It is ideal for edging borders, ranging in height from 6 to 15 inches.

ANTHEMIS (golden daisy) — If you're partial to yellow, you certainly will enjoy growing the golden daisy, or anthemis in your garden. Kelwayi Yellow is the best variety. From June until frost it freely produces slightly aromatic, pure golden-yellow daisy-like flowers carried on long stems which are fine for cutting. You will find the plants grow extremely well in sandy or dry soils, but remember they like sunny locations. Average height is 2 feet.

ACHILLEA (yarrow)—Not too many gardens contain the attractive achillea. It's a wonderful perennial for cutting and adds a tremendous amount of charm and beauty to the middle of the perennial or mixed

border. If you're lucky enough to have a special cutting garden, a half a dozen plants of this attractive perennial would be an extremely worthwhile addition to it. The blooms can be dried and used as indoor bouquets which last many weeks indoors. The plants grow 2½ to 3 feet tall and produce clusters of small, double chrysanthemum-like flowers from June to the end of September.

Achilleas can be bought as plants from your local nursery or garden center, or can be grown from seed. If you plant the seed in a fine sandy soil indoors during March, then set the plants out early in May, you could probably have flowers the first year. Seed set outdoors in May and transplanted in September will bloom the following Summer.

AQUILEGIA (columbine)—In the past twenty years, our plant hybridists have greatly improved the aquilegia, or long-spurred columbine as it is usually called. This attractive perennial is native to a great

part of North-Eastern North America and can be relied upon to flourish provided the soil is kept moist and its position shaded. Experienced home gardeners regard the aquilegia as being one of the most charming and graceful perennials in existence. It's a thrill to see it in flower, whether growing wild in the woods, or in someone's mixed or perennial border. Flowering time is May to July.

Flowers of this outstanding strain average 4 inches in diameter, and if well-grown will be closer to five inches. The colour range includes blues, pinks, maroons, purples, red, deep yellows, primrose yellows, and showy combinations of these colours.

Since the strong free-flowering plants grow 2½ to 3 feet high, they should be planted towards the back of the border.

The traditional columbine spurs protruding from the back of the flowers are exceptional, being widely flared and growing 3 to 4 inches in length.

McKannas Giant can be sown from seed. Spring or early Summer sown seed will product plants ready to be set out in permanent positions in September. The following Spring you will be thrilled with the abundance of flowers.

Mrs. Scott Elliott—strain is also outstanding and produces a marvellous array of splendid colours ranging through shades of lavender, orchid, mauve, blue, purple, yellow, pink, and red. Each plant produces masses of flowers, many of which are bi-coloured.

Red Riding Hood—Flowers are composed of a mixture of old rose and pure white. The spurs are so short that they are practically hidden, but the plants are very prolific bloomers. This variety does not grow quite as tall as the others, averaging 2 to 2½ feet in height.

ARABIS (rock cress) — These are showy, dwarf, spreading border and rock plants which grow from 8 to 12 inches tall. They need a sunny location, and a well-drained soil. The arabis produces masses of bloom in the early Spring. Late April and early May is the normal flowering season.

Single White Arabis

AUBRETIA—(purple rock cress). Here is a delightful perennial for the front of the border, covering spaces in the rock garden, for planting along the top or side of a stone wall, or the front of the foundation planting. Aubretia is one of the very finest of the dwarf spreading perennials. Masses of rosy purple-pink, blue and lilac blooms produced in late April and early May are enhanced by the silvery green foliage. It will grow fairly well in semi-shade, but prefers a location in full sunshine. The new large-flowering hybrids are the best varieties to buy. Aubretia must be divided every two or three years after they have finished flowering, otherwise it will spread out and cover the entire border.

Aquilegia is one of the most graceful perennials in existence

Chrysanthemums come in a wide range of colors

CHRYSANTHEMUMS — Next to annuals the hardy chrysanthemum is one of the most useful flowers to grow in the garden. Unfortunately you cannot plant these heavy flowering plants and neglect them to the same extent as petunias or marigolds.

You will find many uses for "mums" as they are commonly and affectionately called. Try planting them in blocks down the front of the perennial border for a late season big splash of colour and bloom, or use low-growing varieties in the spaces of your rock garden. Planted against the background of shrubs and evergreens you can create a colourful garden picture of unexcelled beauty. Other suitable spots are either on a gently sloping bank, or along the bottom of a rock wall.

Chrysanthemums are quite flexible, you can move them when in bud or even in full bloom without hurting the plant one little bit. This advantage can be exploited with wonderful results in your garden. A good idea is to plant a group of mums in an out-of-the-way spot in the garden and let them grow there until just before they come into flower, then you can move them to the foundation planting, to window boxes or if you live in a spot where the frosts come early you can pot them up and take them inside the house or greenhouse and get up to six weeks more bloom.

With so many uses, why aren't chrysanthemums grown by the average gardener? The answer to this question lies in the fact that so many people give mums a try and get poor results because they never bothered to find out the few simple steps necessary to get good results. First of all you must realize that while the chrysanthemum is a perennial you don't treat it like one. The only way you can get good results each year is to start with a small rooted cutting. Plants that have been carried over from last year's garden need dividing every Spring. Dividing should be completed early in the Spring, but even if left a little later you can still expect plenty of bloom in the Fall. Select your cuttings or division from the outside of the clump. Each one should carry a single stem with roots attached.

If you are buying plants for the first time, buy newly started plants from pots or plant squares, but don't be in too big a hurry to plant them out in the garden. Chrysanthemums never grow well while the days are hot and the daylight is long. You can plant up to the middle of June and have a good show of bloom in the late Summer or Fall.

ARMERIA—(sea pink) (6 inches to 2 feet). If you are looking for the fool-proof perennial, this very fine plant will really fill the bill. Plants are most attractive and have dwarf, tufted foliage, above which rises many stiff wiry stems topped with lovely dense, globe-shaped flowers. The armeria is useful in the rock garden, for edgings, makes a fine cut flower and adds beauty to the front of the mixed or perennial border.

Glory of Holland — (giant pink) is an ever-bloomer which produces flowers in quantity all Summer long. The clear, deep pink flowers are carried on straight stems growing 24 inches in height.

Formosa Hybrids feature large flowers in a charming mixture which contains the deepest to lightest shades of pink, rose, coral and light tones of red. Grows 1½ to 2 feet tall.

Laucheana — Often called the pincushion plant. Growth consists of a compact mound growing six inches high covered with fragrant flowers a rich, silvery pink in colour, and borne on stiff stems. This is a particularly hardy variety. Flowering time is May and June.

Armeria Laucheana is often called the pincushion plant

Any location in the garden where the sun shines for at least two thirds of the day will be satisfactory. Any soil that will grow good garden vegetables will also grow fine mums. Regardless of the fact that your soil is heavy or light the preparation is the same. Before planting work a quantity of peat moss into the soil. Use enough to make the soil at least one-third peat moss and work it down to a depth of eighteen inches for best results. When it comes to planting time, dig a hole much wider and three inches deeper than needed. In the bottom of the hole place a small handful of complete fertilizer or plant food, then cover this with two inches of soil to build the level of the soil up to planting depth and also to make sure the roots do not have direct contact with the fertilizer, or burning of the roots can result.

Plants started in plant squares or clay pots should be set in the hole so that the top of the ball of soil surrounding the roots is one to two inches below the surface of the surrounding soil. Spread the roots out evenly on all sides and cover with two to three inches of the soil and peat mixture. Firm this well around the roots to get rid of the air pockets. Then fill the hole up with water and let it drain away before adding the remainder of the soil.

After the new growth has reached six inches in height, it is time to make your first pinching. Pinching is a very simple but extremely necessary operation in the successful growing of chrysanthemums. Merely pinch off one or two inches from the growing tip of the plants. By doing this you will force the plants to produce side growth and become stocky and bushy. Just as soon as these new side growths have reached about eight inches in length, pinch all of them in the same way. In early July it may be necessary to pinch again in order to produce really husky plants.

Hardy chrysanthemums are most useful in the garden

Pom Poms have honeycomb-like, globular blooms

37

Watering is very important. Water once a week, making sure the water penetrates to a depth of seven to eight inches. The best way to water is to dig a small furrow around the plant at the outer spread of the branches. Make the furrow a couple of inches wide and deep. Fill the trench with water two or three times at each watering until the water is absorbed slowly by the soil. Refill the soil the following day.

It won't be necessary to feed the young chrysanthemum plants. Wait until the first of August and then give them a feeding with a complete fertilizer or plant food. A small handful spread carefully under and beyond the outer spread of the branches and worked into the soil will do the job nicely. Just as soon as mums start growing give them a dusting or spraying once a week with an all-purpose insecticide and fungicide which contains the two chemicals, malathion and phaltan. Dust or spray your mums whether they appear to need it or not.

Once these delightful plants burst into bloom they require plenty of water, whether you have them planted out in the garden or potted in the house. You will probably find that at this stage of their growth they will need watering every other day.

Before you buy, be sure and check your local nurseryman's catalogue for the varieties best suited to your area. The average cost of the rooted cuttings is not high, the price varying from thirty-five to fifty cents per plant, with cheaper prices if you buy in quantities.

Any of the chrysanthemum varieties listed under the All-America label are outstanding. To win an All-America award a variety must be better in its colour and class than any previous variety, you can therefore buy them with confidence and at the same time know that these have been bred for modern times and for every home to grow and use.

Mums need a lot of water from the time the buds appear

2 WEEKS   3 WEEKS   12 WEEKS   NOT PINCHED

After the new growth is 6″ high it is time to make the first pinching

Harvest Giant Mums develop low spreading plants

petalled, not flat or thin like the usual garden chrysanthemums.

Under normal garden conditions, Harvest Giants will develop spreading low plants which vary in height from 18 to 30 inches depending on the variety and the treatment. Some varieties require staking.

COREOPSIS—This fine gay plant has always been one of the most popular and easy-to-grow perennials for the garden. Unfortunately, in the years before World War II, no new varieties were developed, and so the coreopsis lost a great deal of its popularity.

During the past ten years, plant breeders have made so many improvements that you can now have golden yellow coreopsis blooms from June until Autumn.

The main secret in keeping the coreopsis flowering, is *never to let any of the blooms go to seed.* Coreopsis will produce flowers the first year if the seed is sown indoors during March or early April. The plants make a fine show when planted in the middle of the border, and also are worthy of a place in the cutting garden. They grow most vigorously and are very drought resistant.

Coreopsis plants will do well in any type of soil, but grow to perfection in a moderately fertilized light loam. Give them a location in the garden where they'll get as much sunshine as possible. Coreopsis and most other perennials are best planted in groups of three in the form of a triangle, with the base of the triangle being closest to the back of the border or bed.

HEUCHERA (Coral Bells) (12 to 18 inches)—One of the daintiest perennials for the front of the border, foundation planting, or pockets in the rock garden. This is a neat growing and graceful flowering perennial which yields an abundance of flowers that are fine for cutting. Coral Bells are also very effective as edgings to walks. They should be planted in fairly rich, well drained soil in a sunny location. Plant 6 inches apart and divide every third year for best results.

Bressingham Hybrids — These new English Hybrid heucheras have a beautiful range of colors. The shades vary from white to pink, to coral and red in a charming combination of tints. Flowers are excellent for cutting and unsurpassed in the garden where their graceful airy display never fails to draw attention. They are perfectly hardy and have evergreen foliage.

HARVEST MUMS — For many years home gardeners have wanted a really giant "football" type of chrysanthemum that would bloom in their gardens in the Fall without too much attention on their part. Greenhouse varieties flowering in November are too late to beat the frosts in all but the warmest areas. The Harvest Mums solve this problem beautifully.

Many of the harvest mums will be in full bloom by mid-September. The cycle continues with four others flowering by late September, and the largest by early October.

The Harvest Giants are sold by leading nurseries and garden centers. Their flowers are really large, most of them varying from 4 to 6 inches in diameter, with a few measuring seven inches or better. Blooms are really the football type and are deep and heavily

39

DAYLILIES — Hemerocallis — The daylily has come into its own during the past two decades. Most perennials are easy to grow, but none is easier than the daylily, yet no flower is more beautiful. They never seem to be attacked by either insects or diseases. Beginners to this wonderful hobby of gardening would do well to choose the daylily as their first perennial, for these attractive long blooming plants don't need pampering the least bit. They usually bloom two or four weeks. Daylilies will grow in either full sun or light shade, and in any part of the country. They do not require any special kind of soil, but will grow in lime or acid, clay or sandy soils.

Soil conditions don't need to be nearly as good for daylilies as they would be for tall and vigorous growing plants like delphiniums. On the other hand, you should aim to give them the best type of growing conditions possible.

The preparation of the soil will be the same whether it is heavy or light. First of all, spread humus over the soil at the rate of six bushels per hundred square feet. Materials processed from sewage, peat moss, well-rotted barnyard manure, discarded mushroom manure, compost or leaf mold are all good forms of humus. On top of this scatter a complete plant food or fertilizer at the rate of 4 pounds per 100 square feet. Dig this into the soil making sure that the earth, the fertilizer and the humus are well mixed together. From them on no further feeding will be necessary except for a sprinkling of complete fertilizer early in the Spring and again after the flowering season is over. Do not feed with a complete fertilizer in the Fall, as this will stimulate late growth and the plant will not be able to withstand the cold weather just ahead.

Planting time is either very early in the Spring or in August or September when the flowering period is over. A good plan would be to visit nurseries or gardens in the Summer and see the daylilies in bloom so you will be able to choose the varieties you wish for planting in late Summer or early Fall.

A few daylilies can be grown from seed, but normally plants are obtained by dividing the existing roots after the blooming season is over. In this way you can be assured you get the colors selected.

The depth you plant is important. Set the crown no more than one inch below the surface of the soil. You can easily recognize the crown of the daylily. It is where the leaves and stems join the roots.

Daylilies are delightfully fragrant

Daylilies make fine cut flowers

A fine pink daylily

To get the most from these delightful plants avoid dividing the clumps until they are well established, usually after two to three years growth, and reaching a suitable height. Most beginners tend to divide before the plants are matured enough and in so doing never see the varieties at their best.

You will discover the reds are richer and deeper in color if grown in partial shade, whereas, the pinks are prettier when grown in the full sun.

It is also important to realize that there is a big difference in the size of plants, both in the size of their blooms and in their growth habit. For instance, some flowering size divisions look like a little more than a few blades of grass, while others will be rank and enormous.

DELPHINIUMS (4 to 8 feet) — The delphinium is one of our most stately and colorful flowers. Their massive fascinating spikes of white, blue, pink, purple and lavender are unsurpassed by any other flower.

There is a vast difference in the modern delphinium as compared with those of earlier days. Ask any old-time gardener and he will certainly tell you that the modern hybrids are vastly superior in almost every respect. In earlier days, we were satisfied to have a flower spike four feet tall, half of which would be leaves. Now, six and seven feet spikes are normal with at least four feet being blossoms.

Delphiniums like the soil to be rich and containing plenty of humus and plant food. If you stop to think about it, those six to eight feet spikes of bloom cannot be produced from nothing. When delphiniums are planted in poor soil which contains little or no humus, just as soon as the weather becomes warm in the late Spring the leaves will start to turn yellow and if any flowering spikes do develop, they will be puny ones with small blooms. They certainly would be a far cry from the six to eight feet spikes of color you would normally expect.

Where the soil is on the poor side, as it it in so many of our new subdivisions, the best plan is to dig a hole two feet square and two feet deep and replace this with a soil mixture consisting of two parts good top soil, one part humus and one part sand. To each bushel of this mixture, add two handsful of complete fertilizer.

The right location for delphiniums will be one that gives full sun, and at the same time some protection from strong winds. For the best effect, set the plants 18 inches apart in groups of three in triangular fashion.

Delphiniums are one of the earliest perennials to awaken and show signs of life in the Spring. They will be growing 3 or 4 inches high almost before you are aware of them. It is for this reason that planting should be done just as soon as the soil is workable in the Spring. Usually at their best in their second year, you should not expect too much from the plants during their first season. The first year, it will be just as well to let one flower spike develop and remove the rest.

Established plants like to be left undisturbed, it is therefore advisable to keep well clear of your delphiniums when cultivating the border. Forking or cultivating close to the roots will have a bad effect on their growth. It is enough to lightly scuff the soil around them, at the same time working into the earth a handful of complete fertilizer.

Once the flowers begin to show they will require lots of water. Soak the plants thoroughly every three or four days, unless there

Delphiniums are stately flowers

Just as soon as delphiniums have finished flowering the tops can be pinched out, allowing the side branches to go on flowering.

In securing plants to a stake, make sure the tie is loose enough so that the stem won't be injured

is adequate moisture in the soil supplied by rainfall. The water should penetrate the soil to a depth of at least six or seven inches.

A mulch of peat moss, well-rotted barnyard manure, or compost applied at least two or three inches deep around the plants will help keep the roots cool and conserve the moisture in the soil.

Once the spikes get to be 18 inches high, is the time to stake the plant firmly. A triangle or circle of stakes around each clump is much better than using a single one. Be particularly careful in putting the stakes in place, you can very easily damage the roots of the delphiniums. Remember we said they liked to remain undisturbed as much as possible.

If you like quantity of bloom rather than a few spikes of top-size flowers, allow all the spikes to come to maturity. This will provide the border with a big mass of bloom, and is indeed a very lovely sight. However, if you wish to exhibit the blooms at a garden club, flower show, or just want to see the quality you can get for your own satisfaction, reduce some of your vigorous clumps to about three spikes. Feed early in the Spring, and again just before the buds appear, with a complete fertilizer. Keep the

plants well watered at all times and you will be surprised at the huge flower spikes which follow.

Cut back the plants as soon as they finish blooming, down to about a foot from the ground, give your plants another feeding of complete fertilizer, and a second crop of flowers can be expected in late August or September from healthy two- or three-year-old plants. Do not let one-year-old plants bloom more than once, as it will only retard their development.

The effective life of a delphinium in the garden is about three years. At the end of that time you will either have to replace it with new stock or divide. In most cases the best plan is to replace with fresh stock. However, if a particular clump has better than average color and size of blooms, it will often pay to divide.

Time to divide is in the very early Spring just as soon as the first green leaves and stems poke through the ground. It's not a difficult job; just dig the plants, wash off the soil and cut the clumps apart with a sharp knife. Each division should contain from three to five shoots. Replant immediately in soil that contains a large amount of plant food and humus. Delphiniums are

tall and vigorous growers needing a constant supply of fertilizer and humus.

Growing your own stock of delphiniums from seed is not hard. Make certain you buy your seed from one of the top delphinium growers at the beginning of August. Be sure to specify you want seed from the current year's new crop. *Remember the further you get away from the maturing date of any seed the bigger the drop in germination.* Delphinium seed will germinate far better if the temperature is kept to about 55 degrees F. You may ask how is it possible to keep the temperature that low during the warm days of August. You should be able to come close in the cool of the basement, on the floor, and this means you will have to sow the seed in seedling flats or pots. Seed may also be sown in August in a shaded cold-frame. Best way is to sow the seed in very shallow drills or trenches covering it with no more than one eighth of an inch of soil.

After sowing the delphinium seed, whatever you do don't let it dry out. If you have the seedling flats in the basement you have to keep a careful eye open for the day they start to sprout. Once this happens move the flats outdoors. The best place to keep them is in a cold frame until ready for transplanting. The young plants should be large enough to transplant by early September. The best place to keep them during the Winter is in the cold frame bed. Or you can replant them in seedling flats spacing them about three inches apart. Transplanting should be completed at least a month before frost to give the young seedlings time to become well established. This first Winter they will need covering with a couple of inches of straw or hay to prevent Winter damage by heaving caused by frost.

The most famous strain of the tall growing large flowering delphiniums is undoubtedly the Pacific Hybrids developed by Vetterle and Reinelt in California. In growing these hybrids from seed you'll discover that they only come about 90 percent true to color. Those of you who buy your plants from a nursery or garden center would be well advised to pay a visit at the time the year's new crop of seedlings flower for the first time in August and September. You will be able to mark the colors you wish for planting later in the Fall or early the following Spring. Where the climate permits, Fall planting is better than Spring planting. Delphiniums start to grow much more quickly in the Spring than almost any other perennial and you'll give them quite a set back if you transplant them when the new growth is more than 6 or 7 inches tall.

DICENTRA (Old-Fashioned Bleeding Heart)—It's the truth to say that this perennial beauty has been planted by the millions all over North America. Bleeding Heart has been a favourite in the garden for over 60 years. It's a very hardy perennial that will thrive even in the shady spots.

New plants are obtained by division of the roots. A two to three inch piece of root will soon produce a new plant if set in a rich soil. The best time for dividing is during the Fall.

DORONICUM (Leopard's Bane) is a comparatively unknown perennial with fascinating golden yellow daisy-like flowers. Strangely enough this plant is a member of the thistle family, although you wouldn't be able to tell this by its appearance. The blooms make excellent cut flowers, with very straight stems. The leaves are also attractive, being heart-shaped and a bright green in colour. Flowering time is late April and May which means that it's one of the very first perennials to bloom in the Spring. The plants thrive under average conditions, but

will grow in a much better way if given a soil which contains plenty of humus and fertilizer. To get the best results, be sure and make the soil at least one-third humus. Any one of the following types of humus will be satisfactory: materials processed from sewage, peat moss, well-rotted barnyard manure, discarded mushroom manure, compost or leaf mold. At the same time, work into the soil a small handful of complete fertilizer for each plant. Doronicums will grow well in either a light shade or a full sunshine position.

HOSTA or FUNKIA (Plaintain Lily) (12 to 18 inches) — A happy solution to the problem of what to grow in the shade is provided by plantain lilies. They are a group of the lily family and are known by the botanical names of hosta or funkia. They are permanent and hardy, blooming in late July and August. Flower stems rise a foot or more above the large, glossy foliage, and bear small white, lilac or lavender bells in one-sided clusters. They like a fertilized enriched, deep soil in a moist, shady place, but are most tolerant of poor growing conditions. Plants grow and bloom well either in an open sunny border or in dense shade where few other plants will bloom. For the north side of the house, under trees or other problem spots, they are just the thing.

They multiply, and in old gardens, clumps spreading several feet wide are sometimes found. Roots may be lifted and divided either in Fall or Spring. The heavy mat of roots cannot be separated, but must be cut with a sharp knife.

A few plants of several varieties, or two or three plants of one kind will transform an uninteresting shady spot into one of beauty.

Once established, plaintain lilies need no care. Pests do not attack them, severe cold means nothing to them, and even in prolonged dry weather they will not wilt.

Variegata—This variety produces waxy leaves, handsomely variegated with silvery white. The leaves are often 12 to 18 inches in length and grow in a tight cluster to create a very fine plant. You can use the leaves for cutting as they blend handsomely with other flowers. Flower spikes are about 18 inches high, with clusters of lilac, bell-shaped flowers. Plants can be dug in the late Fall and grown in a shady window where the variegated leaves make a fine show.

Subcordata Grandiflora—Very large, pure white, lily shaped, fragrant flowers burst into bloom in August and September. In some respects the leaves and the flowers resemble those of the trillium. This par-

The leaves of the Variegata strain of Plantain lily are useful for cutting

43

ticular variety is used very extensively as a ground cover for lily beds. The foliage provides the needed protection for the bulbs, and the flowers, because of their lily-like appearance, blend in well with the taller growing lilies.

LINUM (Perennial Flax) — One of the most satisfactory perennials for the beginner and the experienced home gardener to grow in the garden is the perennial flax. It is a distant relative of the flax which the farmer grows to produce fibre and linseed oil. However, the kind we grow in the garden is very different. It is a very beautiful perennial, forming feathery clumps of slender flowering stocks. The glorious light blue flowers appear in profusion from May until August, varying in size from 1/2 to 2 inches in diameter.

Here is a flower that's easy to grow and does not seem to be attacked by any insect pests or diseases. Every day new buds burst into bloom, only to fade by evening. Perennial flax is easily grown from seed and grows well in ordinary soil conditions. Be sure to give it an open and sunny location in the garden. Is best planted towards the front of the border, or used for foundation planting, or in pockets in the rock garden. Grows to a maximum height of two feet.

LYTHRUM (Loosestrife) (2 to 3 feet) —There isn't a better perennial for planting at the back of the border than the lythrum.

This popular perennial is completely hardy does best when planted in full Sun, but grows reasonably well in part shade. It is not the slightest bit choosy when it comes to soil, and has no trouble making a home for itself even in moist or partially wet locations. It can be safely said lythrum is one of the easiest of all perennials to grow, and requires practically no care. Blooms continuously from some time in June until September. After it's through flowering the seeds colour very attractively, and in the Fall, the foliage turns a striking reddish-purple. Plants are bushy and will grow three feet high under good soil conditions.

GAILLARDIAS—There's no doubt that this perennial gaillardia is one of the most desirable hardy plants that can be grown in any garden. Brilliantly colored, long stemmed, large daisy-like flowers are produced in profusion from June until the hard frosts of late Autumn. Gaillardias have a remarkable ability to withstand dry weather conditions and go on flowering well when most other perennials have given up.

It's only fair to say the gaillardia has one fault, it cannot be depended upon to survive the Winter when planted in heavy clay soils. Give it medium or light soil conditions and it will go on thriving year after year.

Just as with other flowering plants, you'll get far more bloom if you prevent the formation of seed heads by cutting off the flowers as they fade.

Gaillardias can be grown from seed, but your best bet is to purchase young plants locally. The hairy foliage deteriorates quickly in shipping parcels or packing cases.

IRIS—One of the first perennials to be planted in any garden is usually the bearded or German Iris. There is good reason for this, they not only provide one of the most spectacular displays of flowers in late May and early June, but there is hardly a perennial that is easier to grow.

Fortunately for us this burst of exceedingly colorful bloom comes at a time when the big display of color given by the daffodils, tulips and the early flowering perennials is either definitely on the wane or over. Furthermore, it is usually produced before the buds of the peonies and roses have begun to show any real color.

Where does the name "bearded" originate? It refers to the beard-like strip of hairy growth on the three divisions of the flowers that usually droop down and are called "falls". We could really call this beard an "Iris lighthouse" because it serves as a signal or guide to bees and other insects seeking nectar, leading them to the store hidden deep in the heart of the flower.

Don't follow the common mistake of making a border 2 or 3 feet wide, then planting Irises in a straight row down the middle of it, for after two years growth the plants will have completely filled the border. Irises growing under these conditions provide two to three weeks real beauty in June followed by a mass of green stalks and leaves for the rest of the year. Irises should be part of the middle portion of the mixed border.

Experience has shown that it does not pay in most cases to accept a gift of a few roots from your neighbour when intending to plant Iris. Why do we say this? There have been so many varieties developed in the past ten years you should first study a catalogue from a reliable dealer, to pick out the colours which will blend with your own garden plan and color scheme.

The right location for Iris is in a spot where they'll get full sun all day long. However, some shade can be an asset when the flowers are in bloom, as it helps to lengthen the flowering period, and stops the colors from fading. In any case, Irises should have

Blue Sapphire iris

at least four or five hours sunshine a day in order to grow and flower well.

The type of soil is not too important, for it can be clay loam on the heavy side, or sandy loam on the light side, well drained soil being the main requirement.

Two or three weeks before planting, work a quantity of humus and complete fertilizer into the soil. Apply the humus at the rate of 6 bushels per hundred square feet, and the fertilizer at the rate of four pounds per hundred square feet. Mix the soil, the humus and the fertilizer thoroughly together. *Fertilizers high in nitrogen should be avoided.*

When is the best time to plant Iris? Actually they are so easy to grow you can plant them any time the soil is workable, but the best time is when the plants are dormant — this occurs from late July and during August. Iris planted during this period bloom the following year.

Irises should not be planted in single file. The old reliable group of three that is used so often in planting perennials is the best to use for Iris. Place them in the form of a triangle, with two Iris at the back and one at the front. The distance apart will depend on whether the particular variety is a vigorous or a weak grower. For the latter you would allow 8 inches between plants, for the vigorous growers, you would need as much as 18 inches. This information should be obtained at the nursery when you buy them. Plants bought from a reliable grower, usually contain planting instructions, follow these carefully — particularly as to spacing. If you made your purchase through the mail, consult your supplier's catalogue or nursery list.

For the first three or four years after planting, the size of the bloom is usually maintained, but after that they diminish in number, quality and size each succeeding year. The answer to the problem is to divide the clumps of Iris every third or fourth

Iris is an easily-grown perennial

Clumps of dwarf bearded iris

year, an easy job which can be tackled by the newest home gardener. This necessary task should be performed during the dormant period which begins just after the flowering period is over and lasts until new growth starts again in September. July is the best time to divide and replant, but no harm should result if it's done during August.

All German Iris are divided and propagated by a simple division of their peculiar form root known as a rhizome. This is really a fleshy underground stalk from which grow the true rather string-like roots. Believe it or not, a rhizome actually travels as it grows. Close examination of the growing end will show that it creeps or moves horizontally while the other end gradually dies.

To divide the bearded Iris, carefully dig up the roots, shake off all soil and then give them a thorough wash. Select healthy firm sections with four arms each to be separated from the old bloom stalks. With a sharp knife, cut the selected sections from the rhizomes. Next, cut half the leaves from the cut away sections with scissors. If all the leaf area is left, there will be too much evaporation of moisture from the leaves and the plants will wilt.

Never pull the rhizomes apart or tear the foliage by hand as the ragged ends will attract insects and disease. Rhizomes suffering cuts or injuries should be exposed to the sunlight for 4 or 5 hours before replanting. Dusting the wounds with sulphur is further insurance against disease.

Divide roots with a sharp knife or shovel

Dig up roots, shake off all soil and wash thoroughly

All hardy asters need dividing early in the Spring

46

MICHAELMAS DAISIES (Hardy Asters)

— Michaelmas daisies are one of the least grown perennials in the garden. This is hard to understand, because these late Summer and Fall flowering plants rival the hardy chrysanthemum with their Fall display of bloom. Furthermore, they don't require half the attention needed for chrysanthemums.

The plant breeders have recently introduced newer and better varieties which deserve attention from the home gardener because they are so easy to grow and are available in such a wide range of beautiful colors. Michaelmas daisies range in height from 6 inches to 6 feet and the flowers vary in width from 1/2 to 4 inches.

There are dwarf types ranging from 6 inches to 18 inches which can be used extensively to add Fall color to the front of the border, foundation planting or large pockets in the rock garden.

The flowering period of Michaelmas daisies starts in August, reaches a climax in late September and often lasts until the end of October if weather conditions permit.

They will grow well in a variety of soils, but particularly like a moist location. For the best results, they should be planted in a well-prepared soil. To get the soil in good shape, dig into it a quantity of humus and complete fertilizer. Apply the humus at the rate of 6 to 8 bushels per hundred square feet, and fertilizer at the rate of 4 pounds for the same area. Set the plants in groups of three in a triangular pattern, with two plants towards the back of the border and one towards the front. Keep the plants at least 12 inches apart. The intermediate and tall-growing kinds will need staking as soon as they reach 18 inches high.

All hardy asters (to which family the Michaelmas daisy belongs) need dividing early in the Spring. Each division should contain 4 or 5 stalks. Don't forget the sharp knife to do the dividing.

Right after dividing, give the plants the first of the four feedings they require each year. A tablespoon of plant food to each plant will be the right amount of each feeding. Scatter it around the base of each plant and gently work it into the soil. Further feedings should be made in June, July and August.

ORIENTAL POPPIES (3 to 4 feet)

— Around the middle of June the garden gets its second wind, for at this time the Irises, peonies, roses and poppies are bursting into

Dwarf perennial asters provide late Summer and Fall blooms

flower. Among this group it's doubtful if there is a plant which will give a bigger show of bloom than the Oriental poppy. These huge, brilliantly colored flowers grow to a height of three feet and more. Being big plants, they need plenty of room. Allow each plant nine square feet of space, toward the back of the border but in front of the tallest perennials, such as delphiniums. Once established, the plants will grow and flower undisturbed for a number of years.

Most people don't realize that they can use Oriental poppies as cut flowers. This can be easily done by dipping the ends of the flower stems in boiling water for three minutes.

They won't need much attention, but it is important to cut off the flowers as they wither. Loosen the soil frequently, but not too close or too deeply around the plants. Experience shows that a garden rake is the best tool to use when cultivating Oriental poppies.

The best planting time is in August or September when they are dormant, although they can be successfully planted in the early Spring before they are more than six to eight inches high. The soil should be well

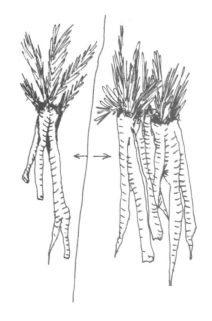

Best time to divide Oriental poppies is in late August or September.

47

drained to prevent water-logging during Winter. When planting, make the hole large enough so that the fleshy roots are not broken or twisted upwards. Water well if the weather is hot and dry, and during the first Winter protect them with a mulch of straw, old hay, or other suitable material.

If you wish to transplant your Oriental poppies to another part of the garden, the time to do it is in August or September, after the leaves have withered. The plants should be dug up carefully so as to damage the roots as little as possible. The best plan is to replant immediately and follow with a thorough watering.

If you grow your own poppies from seed, transplant when they are an inch or so high to flower pots, peat pots or veneer plant bands. This will avoid disturbing the roots.

In growing from seed you may find that the color of the flowers is not entirely true, but there will be a good percentage of the correct color. For the lovely pink shades the best idea is to sow a packet of mixed seed and then mark the color you like.

PEONIES

There's little doubt that peonies are the best all-round perennial for the garden. It also will outlive all others. In New York State there is a 100-year-old peony still growing and flowering well in its original location without ever having been divided or replanted. Felix Crouse is still one of the best double red peonies yet it was first introduced over 100 years ago. They usually grow two to three feet tall and bush heavily.

There are four main types: the single or Chinese, the Japanese, the anemone and the double varieties. Most home gardeners are familiar with the double kinds, but may not know too much about the other types. The single, or Chinese, have flowers with five or more true petals and a center of pollen-bearing anthers. The varieties Krinkled White and Scarf Dance are examples of this group. Mikado and Mme. Butterfly represent the Japanese peonies which have five or more guard petals and a center made up of stamens bearing anthers with no pollen. The anemone group are similar to the Japanese but have no anthers. Typical examples are Philomele and Primevere.

Best time to plant peonies is during the month of September after the weather has turned cool. Early Spring is another satisfactory time but make sure the roots are dormant.

Peonies are the best all-round perennial for the garden

Peonies come in a variety of colors

Causes of Peony Failures
1. Planting over 3 inches deep.
2. Planting in wet, low, or heavily shaded ground.
3. Mulching.
4. Moving plants while growing in the Spring.
5. Planting large clumps instead of divisions.
6. Over fertilization.
7. Crowding by other plants or weeds.
8. Over watering.

Deep preparation of the soil is a must for peonies. Planting holes should be 2 feet wide and a minimum of 18 inches deep. Where soils are poor, it is better to remove all the existing earth and replace it with a mixture consisting of 2 parts good top soil and one part humus. Material processed from sewage, well rotted barnyard manure, discarded mushroom manure or peat moss are the best forms of humus to use. Unless your garden soil is a good one, it is strongly recommended you buy one of the commercial soil mixtures and add the humus to it. Poor drainage can usually be corrected by placing a two inch layer of small stones or gravel in the bottom of the planting hole.

Select clumps or divisions having 3 to 5 eyes. Set the root in the center of the hole so that the *tips of the eyes are exactly 2 inches below the surface of the soil*. It doesn't pay to guess the distance because the most important reason for peonies failing to

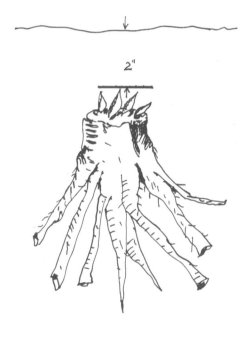

The tips of the eyes of a peony should be exactly 2″ below the surface of the soil

48

A selection of Japanese peonies

Peonies really take over the mixed border for about a month and then there is nothing left but their pleasant green foliage.

For more or less continuous bloom, from late June until frost we have to turn to the tall-growing hardy border phlox which is among the most beautiful of all the garden flowers. Phlox have few needs once they are well-established and during the hot weather of July and August, when many other flowers droop, the phlox will come through in fine style. The perennial phlox is an old garden plant and there are many types and varieties to suit almost any situation and type of soil. Their color range is by far the best and most vivid of any of the perennials.

To grow their best, phlox must be planted in a location where they'll get full sunshine. They will grow fairly well under partially shady conditions, but still need a minimum of 3 to 4 hours a day of full sunshine. Phlox are best planted in the early Spring or Fall, but can be moved even when in full bloom in the Summer. This is especially true and possible when the plants are grown in containers.

The key to successfully transplanting phlox is to dig their future bed at least 12 to 18 inches deep. Deep digging is essential because of the large root growth, and the necessity to make allowance for expansion of the clump. Phlox are also gross feeders and will amply repay any extra feeding you may give them. Before planting, work into the soil a quantity of humus and complete fertilizer. Apply the humus at the rate of 6 to 8 bushels per hundred square feet and the complete fertilizer at 4 pounds per hundred square feet. Mix the soil, the fertilizer and the humus thoroughly together.

Once your plants are established, it is a good plan to give them a feeding with a complete fertilizer just as soon as the soil is workable in the Spring, then follow up with another as the plants begin to bud. This is best done by sprinkling a small handful around the base of the plant and working it lightly into the soil. It is also a good idea to cover the root area surrounding each plant with a mulch two inches deep during periods of extremely hot weather. The mulch can consist of any recommended humus material such as peat moss, compost, materials processed from sewage or grass clippings. This will help to conserve moisture as well as to provide a cooler temperature for the roots.

Like any other plant, phlox should have their dead flowers removed before they go to

bloom is too deep planting. Either use a ruler to measure the two inches or lay a rake handle or piece of wood across the top of the hole and adjust the planting depth so the buds are the width of a man's two fingers from the handle.

It requires two people to plant a peony correctly. Let one person hold the root at the correct planting depth and the other firm the soil around it. Make a thorough job of this to prevent the root sinking after the planting is finished. To make sure this doesn't happen, keep firming the soil around the root until the hole is half full. Then fill the hole with water and move the root gently from side to side as the water is added. Once the water has drained away fill and firm until the hole is filled with soil. Mound up the soil 2 inches high to take care of any further settling. Keep the peonies at least 3½ feet

from other plants.

Fall planted roots will need cover with a two or three inch mulch of hay or straw to prevent the plants from heaving out of the ground during late Winter.

PERENNIAL PHLOX — Permanent plantings in our mixed borders have to compete with the gorgeous blaze of color produced by the annuals. Unfortunately, while most perennials provide a good show of bloom, their display is short-lived covering only a limited period of time.

For example, Oriental poppies give the garden a big burst of color in the late Spring, and then have to be screened from view for the balance of the year.

Delphiniums are spectacular in June and give additional color in September, but for the rest of the year we have just green leaves.

seed. Many people complain each year that their phlox have actually changed color. Originally they planted a lovely red or pink, and now all they get is a washed out pinky-magenta. Of course, it is impossible for the phlox to have changed color. What actually happens is that people allow seeds to form when the phlox have finished flowering, and then these ripen and self-sow. The unfortunate thing about self-seeded phlox is that it reverts to its original color which was once pinky-magenta. The new plants are much more vigorous than the old which have been blooming for a number of years, and so crowd out the original colors.

Don't permit phlox to go to seed. To be sure, keep a close lookout around the base of the plants for any self-sown seedling. If you find any, weed them out. When the flowers start to fade, cut off the entire flowering head, being careful not to remove the leaves with it. These are needed to manufacture food for next year's growth and flowers.

When the phlox clump becomes large and starts to deteriorate, it should be divided. Experience has proven that no matter how good a variety you had in the beginning, in three or four years it will deteriorate and need lifting, dividing, and replanting in good soil. This is best done in August or early September. Divide each clump into sizeable pieces, each with a good mass of roots attached. Cut these from the outside of the clump and throw away the center or old crown as it is usually worthless, woody and diseased.

Perennial phlox usually experiences trouble from an insect called the "red spider", which is really a mite, and the fungus disease, mildew. The red spiders form mealy webs on the undersides of the leaves from which they journey forth to suck the juices from the leaves, and it is not long before these turn yellow and die.

Mildew shows up in the form of a distinctive white haze on the surface of the leaves, and spoils the entire appearance of the phlox plant. The easiest way to control either the red spider or the mildew is to dust the phlox plants regularly once a week from late Spring until the first of October with an all-round insecticide and fungicide containing the new wonder chemicals, malathion and phaltan.

It is not absolutely essential to mulch perennial phlox for Winter protection pur-

poses, but if you plant in the early Fall, be sure to apply a 2 to 4 inch mulch of hay or straw, or some other similar material just as soon as the ground freezes solidly. This will prevent heaving by the alternate thawing and freezing of the soil during thaws in the late Winter and early Spring.

Carpet phlox should be planted in clumps

PHLOX SUBULATA (Carpet Phlox) (4 to 5 inches)—Carpet phlox is one of the most useful of the early Spring-flowering perennials. During the flowering season in April and May the plants are completely hidden under masses of blooms. It is an excellent plant for the front of the border, foundation planting, or in pockets in the rock garden. It also is invaluable as a ground cover for bare spots on the sides of slopes.

All carpet phlox varieties should be planted in full sun. In shade they won't last more than a year or two at the very most.

HARDY GARDEN PINKS — Flowers, foliage and fragrance can be yours by growing the hardy perennial pinks (dianthus) in your garden.

The brilliantly colored flowers are wonderful for planting in beds, borders, rock gardens and in the cutting garden. Plants are quite low growing and range in height from 10 to 18 inches producing blooms which have many different forms and sizes.

About the only care they require is to reduce the size of the plant clumps every year, or in some cases every second year. Once the flowers have faded, they should be removed to prevent the energy of the plants going into producing seed instead of developing next year's blooms.

Dianthus Plumarius (The Grass Pink) is one of the best varieties to grow. This is the old-fashioned, English hardy pink used by the hundreds of thousands in the rock gardens and borders of Great Britain. The smooth, whitish foliage forms in quite thick mats. Two or three, double or semi-double, highly fragrant flowers are carried on each 18 inch stem. There is a wide range of colors including rose, pink, purple, lavender, white and many in-between shades. You'll like the way each petal is delightfully fringed. Flowering time is from early June until mid-Summer.

Grass pinks are easily grown from seed which germinates in less than a week. They prefer a rich, well drained soil, but they'll thrive in almost any sunny location where the soil is well drained. Removing the blooms as they fade will help considerably to prolong the flowering season.

Hardy garden pinks provide flowers, foliage and fragrance

Dianthus Deltoides (The Maiden Pinks) have been favourites for a long time. This is another mat-forming kind having growth which is turf-like. Attractive, fragrant, rather small flowers are profusely produced on stems growing 8 inches high. Flowering time is June and early July. There are two types, Dianthus Deltoides with rose pink flowers, and Dianthus Deltoides Brilliant with blooms of crimson-red. The latter is by far the best variety to grow. Plants of both kinds are vigorous growers and have to be ruthlessly cut back to a small clump 6 to 8 inches in diameter after the flowering season is over.

Allwood's Pink (Dianthus Allwoodi) is a hybrid strain, resulting from crossing the Grass Pinks with Hardy Carnations like Grenadin Red. This particularly fine strain of pinks will bloom steadily from early June until freeze-up time. Plants of this variety will often be in bloom from early June until the middle of November. Clove-scented, double, semi-double and single flowers are freely produced in a wide range of colors, some having attractive and different-coloured centers. Plants grow to an even 12 inches tall.

Dianthus Caesius Splendens (Cheddar Pink) — Another mat-forming pink whose blooms are carried on top of 9 inch stems. Sweet scented, bright pink, daintily fringed flowers are freely produced in May and June. Even when the plants are not in bloom, the foliage is attractive at all times.

Dianthus Cruentus (Red Cluster) This is a tall growing pink which ranges from 15 to 18 inches in height. Many dark crimson-scarlet, semi-double to double flowers are thrown up in clusters from early Summer until freeze-up.

Dianthus Loveliness is an improvement of the original English strain. Colors range from white, mauve and blue to deep crimson. This marvellous range of color combines with the misty effect of the petal to produce a mass of exquisite color in the border. Loveliness is particularly pleasing because of its delightful fragrance. Plants range from 9 to 15 inches in height, but do not require staking.

PLATYCODON (Chinese Bell Flowers) (2½ feet) This is one of the most satisfactory and favourite perennials for the

Chinese bellflowers are a member of the bluebell family

garden. It's a member of the bluebell family and obtainable in showy white or blue varieties. Plants are very hardy but prefer a location in the garden where they'll get plenty of sunshine. The broad blue or white, bell-shaped flowers appear all Summer long.

Good drainage is a must for the platycodon and light sandy soils are definitely the best. Where you're not sure of the drainage, it pays to raise the level of the soil 5 to 6 inches above the general soil level. Avoid transplanting wherever possible.

SHASTA DAISIES (15 to 30 inches) — Here we have a group of wonderful single and double-flowered plants for the center and back of the mixed border. The single flowered varieties resemble giant white daisies and have a large yellow center. The double kinds are like the double-flowered chrysanthemums in size and shape. They not only provide great beauty out in the garden, but are unsurpassed as cut flowers for the house. They need a location in full sun, and the soil particularly for the double varieties should be well-drained.

Wirral Supreme — This is a superb double hybrid shasta daisy originally coming from England. Glistening, double, pure

white flowers are carried on strong two-foot stems. It cuts well and lasts a long time afterwards. Blooms in June and July and all Fall if kept cut.

Double Mount Shasta — Pure white, 100% double flowers appear in quantities from June to October. The long lasting flowers on 15 inch stems are perfect for cutting. This variety must have a well-drained location.

Alaska — A very outstanding variety with extra large single pure white flowers which appear all Summer long. Terrific for cut flower purposes, and absolutely no doubt about its hardiness.

THYME is what might be called a fugitive from the herb garden, because it's also just as fine for planting in clumps down the very front of the border, foundation planting, in pockets in the rock garden or between patio stones. It belongs to the group of six herbs which the French call "les fines herbes."

Most varieties of herbs grow no more than six inches high and so make very fine low-growing perennials that are worth including in any garden for the beauty of their flowers

51

alone. Each plant produces attractive flowers, foliage and tight little woody stems. In addition the fragrant leaves find a ready use in cooking many kinds of delectable dishes.

The various thyme plants are not the slightest bit particular as to soil, and also do well in hot, dry locations. The flowers are produced in June and July and develop into quite a show when well established.

VERONICA (Speedwell) (10 inches to 36 inches) — For a while the veronica faded from public favour, but now that new varieties are being developed, they are practically a "must" for the border, or a rock garden. Veronicas grow well in ordinary soil, and like a sunny location. Plants should be set 8 inches apart in groups of three, in the shape of triangle.

Care of perennials

Watering

More mistakes are made with watering than almost any other job around the garden. Frequent sprinklings every day are not only harmful and stimulate the development of fungus diseases, but they are completely inadequate. By merely sprinkling the surface of the soil you encourage the roots to form near the surface and you damage the flowers.

Watering must be thorough and the moisture should penetrate the soil to a depth of 6 to 8 inches. The best way of making this happen is to use one of the plastic or canvas soakers which slowly lets the water soak into the soil. Perennials that are in bud or flower should have the soil surrounding them kept moist at all times.

Pest Control

The problem of keeping insects and diseases under control is usually not as big a problem with perennials as with annuals. The best thing to do for the average person or the beginner to gardening is to use one of the all-purpose insecticides and fungicides either in spray or dust form.

Applications of all-purpose sprays or dusts should begin when the leaves have appeared in the early Spring, and should continue once a week until Fall.

Plants that are well-fed are not as susceptible to insects and diseases as those that receive little or no plant food. Another im-

A white picket fence makes an effective background for some well grown iris

portant factor in keeping disease and insects under control is the waging of a regular sanitation program. This would include cutting and burning of all diseased plants and debris, and making sure that you only plant healthy plants.

BIENNIALS

BIENNIALS

All about biennials

Biennials are plants which are started late in the Spring or early in the Summer of one year for bloom the following Spring or Summer. Like annuals, they bloom for the one season only, and once their flowering period is over they die.

Forget - me - nots, Canterbury bells and Siberian wallflowers are typical examples of true biennials. However, there are a number of plants which are technically classed as perennials in locations where the Winters are mild, but in the colder parts of the country are so short lived that they are best handled as biennials. Violas, pansies and foxgloves are typical examples of flowers that fall into this category.

Each year many beginners to gardening complain that the Sweet William plants they purchased in the Spring were dead by July. Of course, this is the natural course of events. The plants were sown about the middle of the previous summer, have flowered and produced seed, thus ending their life cycle.

Many readers may say that some of their biennials survive from year to year, and this certainly does seem to happen. However it is not the original roots which survive — the new plants are self sown from the previous year's seed, particularly in the case of hollyhocks and Sweet William. The resulting plants are hardly worth keeping as the seed will not produce plants true to the original variety or color.

You may say "why bother with biennials at all, it is much more convenient to plant either annuals or perennials." This would be a serious mistake because we would be depriving our mixed borders, beds, foundation plantings and rock gardens of some of the most charming flowering plants. It is the biennials that relieve the monotony of the annuals and make possible a much wider choice of flowering plants. A mixed border without clumps of Sweet William towards the front of it, some Canterbury Bells planted in the center portion, and tall foxgloves and hollyhocks at the back would have much less color and beauty.

Pansies flower early in the Spring

How to grow biennials

The home gardener has two ways of adding biennials to his garden. He can buy plants from the nursery either in the Fall or the following Spring. These will then bloom and die after the flowering period is over. The other method is to start them from seed in a cold frame, seedling flat or pit, or to sow them outdoors in the garden.

The question of whether to start plants yourself or to buy them already started from your nurseryman is best decided on the basis of how much fun you get out of growing things and how many plants you need. If you like the feeling of accomplishment, which comes when you say "I started those apricot Violas myself from seed," of course you've become a true gardener. Often you will be unable to buy plants of a fancy new variety, in such cases it would be better to do the job yourself. Or, if your garden is large and you need dozens and dozens of plants, you will find that starting the seeds yourself will give you a very large number for a small investment.

There is a possible third method of starting biennials in February for bloom the same year, but the results will not be as good as those started in the previous season, with two exceptions. Violas and pansies, which we said earlier were tender perennials but treated like biennials, will flower profusely from the middle of August until freeze-up time if the seed is sown in March or April. In the years when the Winters are mild until Christmas, still further bloom can be obtained by placing a cold frame over the plants.

Growing biennials from seed — The majority of biennials are best sown in the early Summer in flats or directly in a seed bed out in the garden. In sowing seeds in regular seed flats (small wooden boxes such as fish flats) prepare your planting mixture by combining one third sand with two thirds soil. Vermiculite may be used instead of sand. It is not necessary to provide an extra rich mixture for starting plants as they will germinate just as well without too much fertility in the soil, and at the same time the danger of fertilizer burn is avoided. Fill the container to the top, and then press down the moist soil firmly with a board. Whatever you do, don't pound the soil in

Pansies should not be allowed to go to seed.

order to make a level seed bed.

Take a pencil and draw shallow furrows or rows 2 inches apart and plant the seed in these furrows. If the seed is very fine it is better not to cover it at all, or with only the finest posible sprinkling of vermiculite or soil. Larger seeds are covered up to three times their narrowest diameter.

Water the newly planted seedling flat by setting it into an inch or so of water and letting it soak up through. As soon as moisture shows on the surface, remove the container from the water, lay a pane of glass across the top to prevent excessive evaporation and to maintain the temperature. Then cover the pane of glass with a sheet of newspaper or a piece of burlap bag. It will probably be unnecessary to water the container again until after the seeds have germinated.

A cool basement or storage shed is the best location for the seedling containers until germination starts to take place.

After the first three or four days, the wisest plan is to check the seedling flats or container daily to see if the seeds have started to sprout. When this happens, remove the burlap or paper and the glass cover. If left on, the newly germinating plants would become leggy and be particularly susceptible to a fungus disease commonly called "damping-off." From this time on, water only frequently enough to keep the soil moist and give the plants

plenty of full sunshine.

Just as soon as the seedlings begin to develop two to four sets of leaves they should be transplanted to another flat, spacing the plants two inches apart each way, or to small individual peat pots, clay pots or veneer plant bands.

A good soil mixture at this stage would be one consisting of two parts good top soil, one part humus and one part sand. Commercial African Violet mixtures available from garden centers, nurseries, and hardware or department stores is a most suitable soil mixture for this purpose. The average gardener or the beginner will probably find it easier to buy one of these commercial mixtures rather than going to the trouble of making up his own.

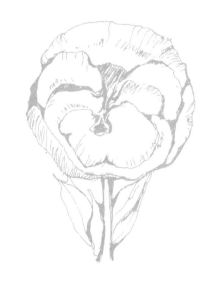

Biennials are an important part of any garden

most people. Very fine seeds should receive no covering or at the most a very fine sprinkling of vermiculite or soil. For the larger seeds, cover them with vermiculite or fine soil to a depth which equals three times their narrowest diameter.

The best way to get fine soil is to run some good garden topsoil through a piece of fly screen.

After covering, tamp the seed gently with a flat board to make sure there is close contact between the soil and the seed.

During the germinating period, it is essential not to let the soil dry out, otherwise many of the seeds will not germinate. However, the waterings should be carried out most carefully, using the finest spray of water possible.

When the seeds are sown, the bed or cold frame should be shaded to prevent high temperatures drying out the soil too quickly. A lath screen set on four wooden legs, 18" to 24" high will provide the right kind of

Once the plants have reached two inches in height there are two steps possible depending on the type of Winter experienced in your area. In locations where the temperature seldom falls to zero or below, the best method is move the biennials to individual clay pots, peat pots or veneer plant bands. Later on when they have formed good clumps, move them to the location in the garden where they are to bloom.

Where the Winters are cold and the temperature frequently falls to much below zero the plants should be transplanted to a cold frame, spaced 6 to 8 inches apart. The cold frame, with a window sash over it and a 2 inch straw or hay mulch covering the plants at freeze-up time, will ensure the plants surviving the Winter in good shape, ready to be moved to the garden just as soon as the soil is workable in the Spring.

Seeds can also be sown in a specially prepared bed in the garden or in a cold frame. Here again a finely pulverized seed bed is essential for good germination. You dig the soil to a depth of six to eight inches and at the same time thoroughly mix into it a quantity of humus at the rate of six bushels per hundred square feet of cold frame or bed area and a complete fertilizer at the rate of four pounds per hundred square feet. For humus you can choose any one of the following and expect success: materials processed from sewage, peat moss, well rotted barnyard manure, discarded mushroom manure or compost.

After mixing the soil, the fertilizer and the humus together, be sure to finely pulverize the soil and make a smooth and level surface. This is best done with a garden rake.

The seeds can either be broadcast over the soil, or sprinkled in shallow rows. The latter method is the easiest and the best for

Sweet Williams

56

shade for seedling beds out in the garden. A similar lath screen without legs can be used if the seeds are sown in the cold frame. Remove the screen when the seedlings are an inch or so high.

In locations where the Winter is severe, the seedlings are best kept in a cold frame which will protect them from frost and excessive moisture during the Winter.

Where the Winters are milder·and the temperature only occasionally falls to the zero mark, the plants can be set out in the garden where you wish them to grow. This is usually done when the plants have formed good clumps, 3 to 4 inches high. A Winter mulch of hay, straw or vermiculite 2 to 3 inches deep should be provided and applied at freeze-up time.

Foxgloves

There is always room for a few vegetables in the flower garden

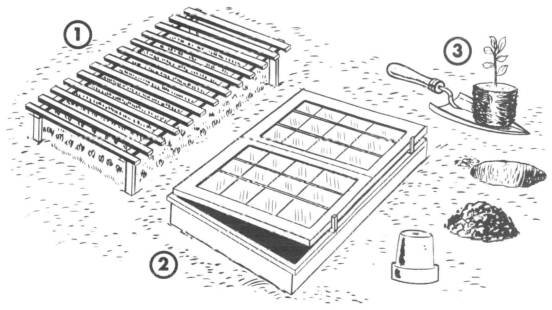

① Sow seeds in early summer in flats for bloom the following year

② Transfer seeding to the cold frame to protect them from frost

③ Remove biennials from cold frame just as soon as soil can be worked

Most popular biennials

Excelsior strain of foxglove is outstanding

FOXGLOVE or DIGITALIS

There are all degrees of patience when it comes to home gardeners. Some just cannot wait at all; they dash out to buy flowering plants in bloom at the nursery then try to create a flower garden overnight as if by magic.

Some are willing to sow seeds and raise plants to maturity, but Spring to mid-Summer or at the most, early Fall, is the limit of their patience. They stick with annual flowers.

Some, and these are the most patient of all are willing to plant seeds in the Summer knowing the results of their labor will not be seen until the following year.

The rewards of such long-term patience are two-fold. First, it costs less in hard cash to be patient, plants grown from seed cost only a fraction of the amount for started flowers. Secondly, you can plant seeds of plants not normally available as started plants at nurseries and garden centers.

Have you ever seen a foxglove in full bloom? This biennial known also as digilatis, grows 3 to 7 feet high spikes crowded with bell-like flowers. The plants grow stately and erect, rightly earning a preferred place at the back of the border.

Patience is certainly required to produce these magnificent flowers. Seed must be sown in late May or early June for blooming the following Summer, after which like all biennials the plants die. It seems a long

time from late May until the next Summer, but your patience will be rewarded to the fullest when you see the towering spikes of foxglove in bloom.

Foxgloves are sown somewhat earlier than most of the other biennials because it takes longer for them to produce plants large enough to flower the following year.

If you live in an area where sub-zero temperatures are common, foxgloves are best wintered in a cold frame. Perhaps it is better in such cold climates to buy plants very early in the Spring, when the soil is workable, from the local nursery or garden center. Be sure to buy the largest plants possible as this will ensure you get the biggest spikes of bloom.

In warmer areas it is best either to buy or move your own home grown plants to the back of the border some time during October. Plants should be set six to eight inches apart in groups of at least 3 or 4.

By planting in clumps you avoid the mistake of having a row of foxgloves along the back of the border looking like a group of soldiers on parade.

Foxgloves should be planted in good garden soil that is well-drained. Good drainage is particularly important because the crowns remain green all Winter and in wet soils will easily rot. Prepare the soil a week or so before the actual planting by digging in plenty of humus and at the same time working into it a complete fertilizer.

Excelsior Mixed — This is a prize-winning variety of the Royal Horticultural Society of Great Britain. The flowers are distinctly different. They bloom earlier and the larger flowers are borne horizontally all around the stem instead of the usual drooping blooms on three sides only. These valuable characteristics make wider, more showy spikes revealing the pretty markings and contrasting spots inside the flowers. Colors include pink, rose, purple, cream, primrose and white. The flower spikes grow from 4 to 5 feet in height, depending on the soil conditions.

Giant Shirley Hybrids — There is hardly a perennial or biennial with the possible exception of the taller delphiniums which will be able to equal the 6 to 7 feet spikes of these extra fine hybrids. The flower heads are 3 feet long and crowded with big, bell-shaped blossoms. Color range is from white and shell-pink to deepest rose.

Many of the blooms are spotted crimson, maroon or chocolate.

Grandiflora — There is no better choice for the mixed border, the wild garden or a woodland setting than this Grandiflora foxglove. Plants are very hardy and produce two to three-feet spikes in June and July. The fine yellowish flowers are attractively marked with brown spots.

FORGET-ME-NOT (Myosotis)

One of the finest biennials is the dainty blue forget-me-not. For some unknown reason it is a flower which has lost some of its popularity during the past few years. It is hard to understand why this should be, because there are very few other plants having the attractiveness of the glorious sky blue color of the forget-me-not.

There are two ways of handling them. If you are fortunate enough to have a small greenhouse, they can be started indoors during February and will be in flower in the late Spring. For most people, the best plan is to treat them as any other biennial and sow the seed outdoors during July or early August. In late September or early October the plants should be set 8 inches apart in their permanent location in the garden. They are highly prized for beds, borders, foundation plantings, rock gardens, for planting in pots and containers and as a dwarf cut flower.

The plants are compact, and grow about one foot tall. You can make up wonderful combinations of sky blue forget-me-nots with yellow and white violas.

Forget - me - nots succeed best in well-drained soils and a sunny location. The plants you set out in the garden in the Fall will need protecting with a two or three inch mulch of clean wheat straw or hay. In the colder areas where the temperature quite often falls to well below zero, the best place to winter forget-me-nots is in a cold frame. Despite the fact the cold frame would be covered with its glass sash, you still need to cover the plants with the same kind of mulch.

Home gardeners who are not interested in growing their own plants from seed will be able to buy them from garden centers and nurseries. Do not make the mistake of buying plants that have been forced into bloom in a greenhouse or electric hotbed. When you do this the plants are at their very best when you buy them and from then on the show of bloom will diminish day by day. It is better to buy them out of bloom or just coming into bud so you get the benefit of the flowering period in your garden. Like other biennials, once forget-me-nots have finished flowering, the plants will die and they will have to be replaced by annuals.

Royal Blue — Many home gardeners and professional plant growers fail to grow the best blue strain which is called "Royal Blue". Think of the sky when it is at its very bluest, and that is the color of this flower.

Rose—Here is an unusual variety which produces exquisite sprays of delicate rose-pink flowers.

White—Few people realise that forget-me-nots also come in white, which combines beautifully with Rose and Blue strains in the garden or as a cut flower in the house.

Varieties treated as annuals

For Summer bloom there are two varieties of forget-me-nots which are treated as annuals. Seed sown indoors in March will produce attractive plants which will be in flower by early Summer.

Bluebird — The dwarf compact plants grow 12 inches high and are covered with beautiful deep blue flowers which are highly prized for both Summer and indoor Winter flowering.

Palustris Semper Florens—This ever-blooming variety features sky-blue flowers from early Summer until cut down by the frosts in late Autumn.

Tall spikes of foxglove give striking beauty to the back of the mixed border.

Double hollyhocks resemble beautiful roses

HOLLYHOCKS

When you grow these towering plants in your garden you have the pleasure of seeing one of the most ancient of all cultivated flowers, for it was a respected ornamental plant in China far back in the dawn of civilization.

Hollyhocks were garden favourites for generations, but lately have lost some of their popularity. This is unfortunate, for they are not only especially suitable at the back of the border making an excellent background for shorter plants, but are very useful for screening unsightly views, bare walls or fences.

There is hardly a plant in the garden easier to grow. They are what might be called a semi-perennial which we treat as a hardy biennial, and require replacing every two years. Plants grow anywhere from 5 to 9 feet in height, blossoming from July until early September. They bear large wide-open single or double flowers along thick and leafy main stems.

Seed should be sown in a cold frame or a seed bed in the garden in July and set one-half inch deep. Plants are set out in their permanent location either in October or early the next Spring, and should be in clumps of three rather than like a file of soldiers.

Hollyhocks require a rich, well-drained soil, preferably a little on the light, sandy side. In preparing the planting sites, dig in large quantities of humus, 8 to 10 bushels per 100 square feet of bed area will not be too much. Discarded mushroom manure, or well-rotted barnyard manure is the best type of humus to use for hollyhocks. In locations where this is not readily available, materials processed from sewage, peat moss, or material from the home compost heap will make a satisfactory substitute. Hollyhocks need a location in the garden where they will get full sunshine.

About the only real problem that occurs in growing hollyhocks successfully is a rust disease which causes rusting, yellowing and dropping of the leaves. The rust is due to a fungus which produces its spores in little reddish lumps on the underside of the leaves. Yellow areas appear on the upper surface of the leaf and in bad attacks of this disease, the leaves turn yellow and fall from the stems.

To prevent the rust you must practise good sanitation which includes removing and burning the infected leaves as soon as noticed, and the burning of all old stalks and leaves in the Fall. As soon as the leaves come on the plants in the Spring, it is advisable to dust them every week with a fungicide containing ferbam. Do this whether or not the plants appear to be infected.

Double-flowered hollyhocks

The Fordhook Giants are a particularly fine strain whose flowers are very large measuring up to 4 inches across. They are carried on stately spikes 5 to 6 feet tall and are loaded with most colorful blossoms which resemble double carnations or roses.

Carnation Flowered Mixed — This variety produces beautiful large blooms 4 to 5 inches across which resemble a huge carnation. Flowers are extremely double and appear on 5 to 6 feet stalks.

Single Large Hollyhocks — These are more permanent and hardy than the double and grow more like a perennial than a biennial. They are sold in a mixture of colors which range from white, pink, scarlet, yellow to maroon. Plants also grow taller than the double kind and will easily reach 8 feet in height if grown in good soil.

Annual Hollyhock — This is a free-flowering strain which can be grown as an annual and flowered in five months from seed. At the same time it is sufficiently hardy to last for several years. If treated as an annual, sow the seed $\frac{1}{4}$ of an inch deep in fine soil indoors during February or March. Seedlings can then be set out in the garden about daffodil or tulip time and the plants will start to flower in July and continue until late in the Fall. Plants should be set in groups of three in triangular fashion at least 20 inches apart. The annual strain is seldom attacked by rust and you will discover the seed germinates in 10 days to 2 weeks.

ENGLISH DAISY (Bellis)

This double giant daisy is actually a hardy perennial, but is treated either as a biennial or an annual to make it produce large size blooms. The attractive flowers combine with pansies or forget-me-nots for most unusual effects. They are excellent for edgings, the front of borders, pockets in the rock garden, or along walks or walls. Blooming commences early in the Spring and carries through the rest of the season. Height is about six inches.

When sowing your own seeds either indoors or out it is important to set them at the right depth. Care should be observed to given them a covering of no more than 1/16 of an inch, seed will not germinate well if planted any deeper.

Plants grown indoors are ready to transplant to flats when they are 1 inch high, and should be spaced 3 inches apart. Transplant outdoors to six inches apart.

The English daisy prefers a moist well drained soil and partial shade. Where the Winters are not too cold and the Summers are cool, the plants will often last for more than two years.

Hollyhock Double Chamois is artistic and unusual

The English Daisy is really a perennial, but is treated as a biennial.

Monstrosa Mixed — A fine mixture which includes carmine red, deep rose pink, and pure white. This variety grows a little taller than the others and averages from six to eight inches in height.

VERBASCUM (Mullein)

Most people are familiar with the wild verbascum which is found growing in many fields and pastures. These should not be confused with some of the beautiful new hybrids which are now on the market. The leaves are more or less woolly or downy, and the flowers are borne on branched spikes.

Verbascums require a light or medium well-drained soil. Planting time is in October, or just as soon as the soil is workable in the early Spring. Set them in groups of three, 8 inches apart. Once a colony of

these plants is established, they will reproduce themselves. Height varies from 3 to 5 feet, so they should be planted at the rear of the mixed border.

61

Few flowers are more colorful than the Iceland Poppies.

ICELAND POPPIES
(Papaver Nudicaule)

Visitors to famed Lake Louise each Summer are always entranced by the exciting display of poppies against the background of the sky-blue waters of the lake and the snow capped mountains. You may not realize it, but some of that beauty can be yours in the garden by planting the colorful Iceland poppy. These poppies have some of the characteristics of both biennials and perennials, usually living for two or three years instead of only one.

Iceland poppies are charming for planting down the front of the mixed border, pockets in the rock garden, among the evergreens in the foundation planting or in a special cut flower garden. The flowers are ideal for cutting, but must be picked in bud.

Plants form neat compact tufts of bright green foliage. Out of this grow the graceful wiry stems bearing flowers of brilliant colors from early Summer, until the season ends.

Seed sown indoors in March or April or outdoors about the first of May will flower the first season. The average gardener should sow the seed where it is to bloom. If sown indoors, seed should be set in individual clay pots, peat pots, or plant bands to eliminate the necessity for transplanting. When seed is sown in seedling flats and then transplanted to other containers, extreme difficulty is experienced, because little or no soil clings to the roots. Plants grow from 15 to 24 inches tall, bearing fragrant flowers obtainable in charming shades, ranging from white to yellow, orange and red.

CANTERBURY BELLS

This biennial belongs to the campanula family of which most of the other members of this group are perennials. The single types of Canterbury Bells are known as "Campanula Medium". Then there are the "double" and the "cup-and-saucer" Canterbury Bells.

The place to plant them is in full sunshine in the center section of the mixed border. They also have a place between the evergreens in the foundation planting. A few plants set out in the cutting garden will mean attractive flowers for the house, and at the same time you will not have to rob the garden of some of its beauty.

To provide a truly effective show in the border or in the foundation planting, they are best planted in groups of three or even more. Space the plants two feet apart to form a triangle, with one plant in front and two behind.

If your garden soil is well-drained, it is recommended you buy your plants and set them out during the month of September. Then they will be ready to jump ahead when the warm weather arrives the following Spring. On the other hand you will be able to buy plants in the Spring from garden centers and nurseries which will provide a very good show of bloom in June from a late April planting.

It is also very easy to sow seed out in the garden in June as outlined previously in the book, and produce your own plants inexpensively for September planting.

Canterbury Bells set out in September will require a special type of mulch, and it is important you use one which will not pack down to a heavy sodden mass over the leaves. One or two evergreen branches placed over the plants first and then covered

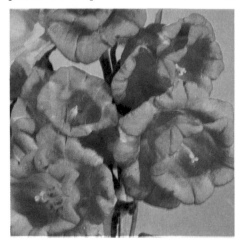

Canterbury bells

with clean wheat straw or hay at least 2 or 3 inches deep makes a most satisfactory mulch.

Incidentally, raked up leaves from shade trees make the worst possible mulch. Don't apply the mulch until the top inch or so of the ground has been frozen solid in late Fall or early Winter.

When buying plants in the Spring, make sure you buy the largest possible because these will give you the most and the largest flowers. Small Canterbury Bell plants do not grow into big plants, as normally happens with most other varieties.

Recommended varieties

Cup-and-Saucer — If you haven't got too much room you will find the "cup-and-saucer" type the most attractive of the three types of Canterbury Bells. The children find this kind most fascinating, because the flowers have a striking resemblance to a cup and saucer. Like the single and double kinds, the cup-and-saucer type produces its flowers in quantity in June. Plants grow from 2 to 2½ feet tall, and the color range is excellent.

Colors are dark blue, light blue, rose and white.

Single Canterbury Bells — The pyramidal plants of this kind grow from 2 to 3 feet tall and flower in June about the same time as the cup-and-saucer varieties. The large bell-like blooms have rolled back edges which are attractively fluted. The color range is the same as the cup-and-saucer type.

Double Canterbury Bells—Plants are covered with double blooms colored white, blue or rose during June, and they grow 2 to 2½ feet in height. They make a very fine cut flower.

SWEET WILLIAM

For over 300 years Sweet Williams have been grown in European and North American gardens. Like carnations and pinks, they are members of the dianthus family. Sweet Williams provide beauty and fragrance for the mixed border, foundation plantings, larger pockets in the rock garden. No cutting garden would be complete without some plants of these free-blooming biennials. If you have a small garden without enough room for both a vegetable and cutting flower garden, you could plant a

There are numerous double and single varieties of Sweet William.

few Sweet Williams in the vegetable section and they will supply plenty of fragrant blooms for the average home.

Flowers in many beautiful colors and combinations are produced in clusters in great profusion, having a pronounced spicy fragrance. There are double and single forms, both of which are equally attractive in the garden, but for cutting the single varieties are best. Each flower is made up of hundreds of miniature rose-like flowers. Seedlings of all double varieties produce about 40 percent of attractive single plants. Sweet Williams bloom at a very convenient time in early June during the lull between the early Spring display and that of the Summer flowers. Plants range in height from 4 to 24 inches.

Sweet Williams demand a soil that is well drained if they are to survive the Winter. Make the soil mixture in which they are to be planted a rich one by digging in plenty of humus accompanied by a liberal feeding of complete fertilizer. Apply the fertilizer at the rate of 4 pounds per hundred square feet and the humus at the rate of 6 bushels per hundred square feet. In poor soils you would be well advised to step up the amount of humus to 8 to 10 bushels per 100 square feet. Any of the following forms of humus will be satisfactory; materials processed from sewage, peat moss, well rotted barnyard manure, discarded mushroom manure or material from the home compost heap.

Sweet Williams are easily grown from seed in late June or July. Seeds germinate in 2 to 3 weeks. You can also buy plants in late September or early October from garden centers or nurseries.

Fall-planted Sweet Williams have to be covered with a mulch as soon as the top inch or so of the ground freezes solidly. It is

The Siberian Wallflower has vivid orange blossoms

most important to avoid using leaves for this purpose as they will form a soggy mass over the plants. Few, if any, plants will be able to survive such conditions. It is better to place one or two evergreen branches over the plants then cover these with clean wheat straw or hay 2 to 3 inches deep.

If you intend to buy Sweet William clumps in the early Spring from nurseries and garden centers, be sure to make your purchases as soon as the plants are available. The sooner you can get them in the ground the better display of bloom you will have in your garden. Plants already in bud or bloom are not worth buying. Not only will the show of bloom be disappointing, but because the Sweet William is a biennial, the plants will die when the flowers fade.

Giant Double Mixed — Plants have a robust bushy habit, producing numerous stems carrying immense fully double flowers. Many of the individual flowerettes measure over 1 inch in diameter. Colors are extremely varied.

Midget Double Dwarf Mixed — This is an attractive dwarf form of the above, growing 3 to 4 inches tall and producing an amazing range of colors.

Single Dwarf Indian Carpet Mixed — This is a 3 to 4 inch Alpine Sweet William whose habit of growth is very compact. Blooms are quite large and almost entirely cover the foliage. Color range is from white, chamois, salmon, scarlet, brick red to maroon. Most of the blooms are tricolored.

SIBERIAN WALLFLOWER or CHEIRANTHUS (Allioni)

Unfortunately the true English wallflower is not Winter hardy in the colder parts of North America. However, many people do get some success with them in cold frames or greenhouses. For compensation we have the Siberian wallflower, a hardy plant best described as a short-lived perennial having small, vivid orange blossoms which continue to flower for a very long period. Flowering time starts with the tulips and adds a bright and cheerful touch to any part of the garden. Grows 12 inches in height.

Seed sown towards the end of June and in early July will produce flowering plants at the end of the following April. The soil should contain a fair amount of humus and plant food, for the Siberian wallflower to grow well.

VIOLAS AND PANSIES

Violas and pansies belong to the class of flowers known as tender perennials and are treated as biennials. They are two of the most useful flowers to grow in the garden. Ideally suited for planting in clumps along the front of the annual or mixed border, foundation planting, along paths and driveways, in window boxes, hanging or supported containers and in spaces in the rock garden. Further, there is hardly a flower, annual, biennial or perennial which will provide as many flowers for the garden or cut blooms for the house over a longer period.

Their colorful blossoms are easily grown and the bright, gay flowers are just as much at home in the city and suburbs as in the country.

Pansies and violas are among the first perennials to flower in the Spring, continuing with their blooms until overcome by the July heat. During the latter part of August when the weather starts to cool, they perk up and commence flowering again and, if the weather remains mild, will stay in bloom until Christmas.

Some people have difficulty in telling the difference between violas and pansies. Years ago it was easy, the pansies had faces while violas were obvious by their clear colors. Today, thanks to the plant breeders, we have clear color pansies without faces and so it is necessary to be something of an expert to differentiate.

Giant yellow violas

Generally speaking, violas are smaller flowered and are more persistent bloomers than pansies.

Both plants are so useful in the garden it is probably best to plant some of each.

There are several ways of obtaining plants, first we will deal with those purchased from nurseries.

Buying Pansies in the Spring — Most people will buy their stock in the Spring and at this time of the year you must be wary of what you buy. Search out a plant grower or nurseryman who grows his violas and pansies outside and has depended on a suitable mulch for protection during the previous Winter. Try to buy his plants when the first blooms are appearing, as in this way you will get all possible flowers.

Beware of violas and pansy plants forced into bloom in cold frames in early Spring, the forcing so saps the strength of the plants that they rarely recover to provide the display of bloom of which they are capable.

Buying Pansies in the Fall — Unless you live in an extremely cold area the better method is to buy the plants from the nurseryman or plant grower in late September and early October and set them out in their permanent locations in the garden. Such plants will need a Winter mulching of hay or straw to prevent them being heaved out of the ground by the thawing and freezing of the ground in Winter and very early Spring.

Growing your own Pansies — If however, you choose to sow your own seed you have two courses of action, sowing indoors or in the garden.

Colorful pansies are easily grown

By planting the seed indoors during March and April the plants will start blooming about mid-August and will continue until freeze-up. As mentioned earlier, during mild Winters the plants will bloom until Christmas. Still more bloom can be produced by placing a cold frame over the plants or by moving them to an unheated greenhouse.

Of all the methods, there is no doubt that sowing seed in the garden during June or July, then keeping the plants until the next Spring and Summer is by far the best way.

Pansies like good soil — The soil in which you plant pansies and violas in the Fall or in the Spring must be a rich one if you wish to obtain an abundance of large blooms. There are many forms of humus which will do a good job of enriching the soil. Many home gardeners are getting real success with one of the humus materials processed from sewage. Other good kinds are well-rotted barnyard manure, discarded mushroom manure, peat moss, material from the home compost heap or leaf mold. Work the humus into the soil at the rate of 6 to 8 bushels per hundred square feet for reasonably good soils, and 8 to 10 bushels

in poor soils. At the same time, spread over the ground, a complete fertilizer or plant food at the rate of 4 pounds per hundred square feet. In very poor soils you could step up the rate of application to six pounds per hundred square feet without any worries.

Finally, mix the soil, fertilizer and humus thoroughly together in the top 8 to 10 inches of soil, and rake level for planting.

The secret to getting more and more blooms is to pick them daily and never let any of the blossoms go to seed. In July, when the sun turns hot, cut the plants back to an inch or two above the ground and give each viola or pansy a feeding with a tablespoonful of complete fertilizer. When the days turn cooler in late August and early September the plants will start giving their second crop of flowers almost as good as the first and which could continue as late as Christmas.

Growing pansies and violas from seed — This is not a difficult task being well within the capabilities of most home gardeners.

First thing to do is to order some top quality seed from a reliable seedsman.

Pansies and violas make a nice edging for a mixed border

Pansies need to be planted in rich soil

Pansy and viola seeds, like delphiniums, quickly deteriorate after the seed is ripe, so it is very important to be sure you are sowing fresh seed from the current year's crop.

Be sure and specify new crop seed when placing your order. An exception to this rule would be pansy and viola seeds packaged in the new Vita-Fresh process which keeps the seed fresh indefinitely.

Violas and pansies under garden conditions degenerate very quickly, this means you cannot save your own seed and get the colors and varieties from which you took the seed.

Success in growing pansies and violas from seed depends on the treatment given the seed in the first one or two weeks after sowing. Once you allow the seeds to dry out after they have started to sprout they will usually shrivel and die. On the other hand, if you keep the soil in which they are sown too damp, the odds are they will get the fungus disease "damping off", and many of them will fail to survive.

Seeds can be sown in pots, seedling flats or in a cold frame. Whichever you use, it must be located where you can control the light and moisture conditions.

The soil mixture must be worked into a fine condition, containing just enough sand to make it slightly on the sandy side.

The best mixture for pansies and violas consists of one part sharp sand, three parts good soil, and one part humus. If you do not wish to make up your own mixture, commercially prepared African Violet soil mixture is satisfactory. Sow the seeds in rows or drills and cover with not more than 1/16 of an inch of soil. Firm the soil very gently afterwards with a flat board.

Before you sow, water the soil thoroughly, and after sowing, give the surface of the soil a light watering.

After a five or six week period, the young seedlings will be large enough to handle and be transplanted to a cold frame where they should be set 6 inches apart or can be planted in the place where they are to flower. The way you handle them at this time will depend on the severity of the Winter. It is most important to remember that each time a pansy or viola root is disturbed, the flowers become smaller.

The time to sow pansy or viola seed is any time from the middle of June to the first of August. Actually it is often advisable to make two sowings—one early and one late. The former will provide lots of September and October flowers.

66

Dried flowers for winter bouquets

Strawflower is a long time favorite, as a fresh cut flower or for drying

Dried flowers, grasses and other plants are very widely used to make attractive indoor flower arrangements during the Winter months. Many of the plants are not only useful for drying purposes, but make excellent fresh cut flowers as well.

The best method to dry flowers and grasses is to cut the material before it is fully developed, remove the foliage, bunch loosely and hang head downward in a cool, airy, shady place. The flowers should be fresh and free from water. Dry them slowly and never expose them to artificial heat.

Seeds of the various plants can either be started indoors in early April or sown out in the garden in early May after the danger of frost is past.

Recommended varieties

Strawflower (Helichrysum) — A long time favorite is the strawflower whose colors include crimson, rose, salmon, yellow and white. Large double flowers often 2½ inches and more across are produced in quantity from the middle of July until Fall. Plants grow 2½ feet tall and the blooms also are equally popular as fresh cut flowers.

Globe Amaranth (Gomphrena) — This is a hardy annual whose clover-headed flowers are very attractive whether they are blooming in the garden or used as fresh or dried cut-flowers. Blooms are produced in quantity and average 3½ inches in diameter. Seed is sold only in a mixture of red, white and pink shades. In addition to being excellent for dried bouquets it will grow well in hot dry locations in the garden where other annuals fail to thrive. Plants grow 1½ to 2 feet tall and should be planted towards the front of the annual or mixed border. Flowers start to appear early in July and continue until frost.

Honesty — Another popular everlasting flower for dried bouquets is an annual called "honesty". It is grown for the silvery white, paper-like, flattened partitions of the round seed pods which when dried are a fine addition to any Winter decoration.

Statice (Sinuata) — One of the very best flowers for drying is the annual "statice". Very pretty clusters of straw-like blooms are carried on stiff stems. Plants produce light and gracefully formed sprays which have unique colorings. Colors are deep rose, pure white, deep blue and art shades consisting of a wonderful mixture of fawn, pink, red, salmon, yellow, orange, white and blue. The sprays of flowers are equally attractive when freshly cut or dried. Plants are easy to grow and reach from two to 2½ feet in height.

Quaking Grass (Briza Maxami) — For the front of the annual or mixed border, an ornamental grass commonly called quaking grass is very decorative and it too can be

The annual statice is one of the best flowers for drying

67

dried for Winter decoration or used as a fresh cut flower. This ornamental grass tenaciously holds its panicles when dried and can be used alone or with dried flowers. The busy plants growing 12 to 15 inches tall bear a profusion of fascinatingly formed, flattened cone-shaped heads.

Job's Tears (Croix Lacryma) is another ornamental grass which will grow well in ordinary soils. It is widely grown for its large, hard and shiny gray seeds which, when dried, are strung as beads. This is an excellent plant to let the children grow, to have the dried seeds for playing with.

Calico Indian — Sometimes called squaw corn and strawberry corn is wonderful for mixing with gourds or for forming separate dried bouquets of their own. The corn is sown in the normal manner when the soil has really warmed up. It takes about 100 days from the time you sow the seed until you harvest the ears. Seed sown around the first of June would be ready for picking about the middle of September.

The kernels of Calico corn are a mixture of various bright colors altogether different to the regular corn.

Strawberry Corn is really a popcorn, but in addition to being excellent for popping, it produces attractive tiny ears which are only two inches long and 1½ inches wide, and these have a most delightful rich and shiny mahogany color. The ears are enclosed in straw colored husks.

Cotton — When cotton is mentioned, we usually think of fields of glistening white bolls growing in the Deep South in the United States. Not many people realize that it can be grown as far north as in southern Ontario, but not commercially. If handled like most annual flowers, it certainly can and is worth growing in the garden.

You start the seed indoors during late March or early April and move to the garden when the danger of frost is past. There the cotton plants will quickly develop into low bushes which have a definite ornamental value, with lovely pink buds followed by the traditional creamy white blossoms. The white bolls will make an interesting and decorative addition to the dried Winter bouquets.

Dried statice makes a delightful flower arrangement

Globe Amaranth will grow well in hot, dry locations in the garden

CUT FLOWERS

Importance of cut flower gardens

A separate cut flower garden sooner or later becomes a must for anyone who really likes to garden.

Where there is no cut flower garden, the lady of the house is forced to rob the brilliant displays of flowers in beds, borders and foundation plantings to provide cut blooms for the house. This is bound to spoil a great deal of the much-needed color they provide in the garden.

The ideal cut flower garden should develop a steady supply of bloom from early Spring until late in the Fall. We should not limit the plants used to annuals, for even if these are started indoors they will not provide any cut bloom until the first of July at the earliest. It will be late that month before sufficient supplies will be available.

The truly successful cut flower gardener makes use of any plant or shrub to lengthen the season and to obtain the utmost variety.

The first blooms would be provided by the early-flowering shrubs such as forsythia and flowering almond. These will provide branches for forcing in January and February. Many of them will flower just as well indoors as outdoors.

First blooms from the garden come from the various Spring flowering bulbs such as snowdrops, scillas, chionodoxas, daffodils and tulips.

Perennials start blooming in daffodil time and with a judicious selection will carry on until frost.

There are also a number of biennials such as forget-me-nots and Canterbury bells, which make extremely useful cut flowers.

Lilies start to flower in June and from then until September they give us some of our most glamorous and exciting cut blooms.

In mid-Summer there are many Summer flowering bulbs such as gladiolus, galtonia, Peruvian daffodil, etc., which give welcome variety to our choice of cut flowers.

Sometime in August and continuing until frost the dahlias provide quantities of colorful cut flowers.

Many annual and perennial flowers and grasses can be dried to give indoor blooms during the late Fall and Winter.

Location & preparation

A cut flower garden should be located where it will receive full sun at all times and some shelter from the prevailing winds.

Its soil should contain lots of humus and plant food. In preparing the soil, dig in a minimum of six bushels per 100 square feet of humus for average soils, stepping this up to 10 bushels per 100 square feet for the poor kinds. Any one of the following types of humus can be used with success: materials processed from sewage, peat moss, discarded mushroom manure, well-rotted barnyard manure or compost.

In addition, a complete fertilizer at the rate of 4 pounds per 100 square feet should be added to the soil at the same time.

The number of plants of each variety will be best learned from experience, although in some cases it will depend on the amount of land available. For all but the annuals, a half a dozen plants of each type should be sufficient in the beginning. For most of the annuals you would probably need a dozen of such kinds as asters, marigolds and snapdragons.

A mixture of flowers makes an effective arrangement

Making cut flowers last longer

Flowers will last and stay fresh for a much longer period if you pick and prepare them correctly. A sharp paring knife will do a much better job of cutting the stems than a pair of scissors. Scissors almost invariably damage or bruise the stems.

In making the cuts, be sure to make them on a slant to increase the amount of cut stem able to come in contact with the water. Naturally this will permit more water to be absorbed by the flowers. The best plan is to take a deep container out into the garden and put the stems into it as they are cut.

Flower arrangements

Talk to any good arranger of flowers and he will tell you that you cannot make worthwhile and attractive arrangements unless you have some basic materials at your fingertips. The first requirement is a selection of flower holders including some of the new plastic types. A trip to your nearest florist can be a big help as the more varied your selection of vases, bowls and other containers, the better.

Before starting your arrangement, do as the professional florist does and remove the foliage that would be under water in your finished arrangement. You will find that leaves which are left below the water will almost invariably start to rot, and so slow down water absorption by clogging the stem.

In any type of flower arrangement, you must have small, medium and tall flowers. One of the most effective ways for the beginner to arrange flowers is to use the right triangle method. One tall flower stands vertically from the container, another flower extends to the side, forming an "L" with the vertical one. In filling in the angle, make sure that the flowers stay close to the "L" framework.

The equilateral triangle is another simple arrangement for the beginner. The framework is formed by three flowers of equal

Sparkler—All-America Gladiolus

length. One is placed vertically in the center. The other two extend horizontally on either side of the center. More flowers are used to fill in the angles to form a solid triangle. This is considered a formal type of arrangement and can be placed on mantels or used as a centerpiece on the dining room table for formal occasions.

A most useful type of arrangement is called the horizontal. The longest stemmed flowers branch out from the sides of the container, parallel to the table. All flowers are close to the top of the vase or bowl, thus making the arrangement low. The horizontal shape is suited for use on low tables or mantels. Because it is low, it makes a good centerpiece for the dining room table.

Under no circumstances do you add water

to the bowl or vase until the arrangement is finished. Then, only add enough water to cover an inch or so of the base of the stems. Your florist will be able to sell you a specially prepared floral preservative which is added to the water. Once your arrangement is finished, leave it alone. Do not rearrange the flowers or change the water. If the water evaporates, just add a little more every day or so.

Thus, a cut flower garden will provide a great deal of outdoor fun and exercise, and present a challenge indoors to make the most decorative use of any of the cut blooms. It is also one of the best ways of interesting children in gardening. They can help grow the flowers, and learn to make their own arrangements.

Gladiolus

Rusty—the first All-America "smoky"

The colorful gladiolus we grow in our gardens come to us from the countries bordering the Mediteranean Sea and from South Africa. Most of the original wild varieties were poorly shaped flowers, but our plant breeders have made tremendous progress in developing gladiolus over the past 50 or 60 years and have produced new varieties with dwarf and tall, in many new colors, all of which are a joy to have in the garden.

The flowers are a source of encouragement to the beginner as they are so easy to grow successfully. The only obvious drawback with gladiolus is that they do not lend themselves too well for use in borders or beds, although some of the new miniature types can be used for this purpose.

Gladiolus will grow well in almost any type of soil provided it has been well supplied with both humus and fertilizer. The location should be changed every year to help reduce the chance of disease.

The preparation of the soil is the same for either heavy clay or light sandy soils. For soils that have been fed regularly with fertilizer and humus, you will still have to apply some more of these materials just as soon as the soil is workable in the Spring. The humus is applied at the rate of six to eight bushels per 100 square feet for average soils, boosting the amount to 10 bushels for poor types. Any one of the following types of humus will be satisfactory; materials processed from sewage, peat moss, well rotted barnyard manure, discarded mushroom manure and material from the home compost heap. The amount of complete fertilizer to apply will be the same for both sandy and heavy soils, four pounds per 100 square feet.

Make sure you buy quality corms from a reliable bulb dealer or seedsman. Corms are available in various sizes making the beginner's choice of purchase a little confusing. Any corm that is an inch and a half or more in diameter will give a good sized spike of bloom. The best size for the average home gardener to plant is the No. 1 corms which vary between 1½ to 2 inches in diameter. Experience shows that the very large flat corms will not flourish as well as the moderate sized ones with the high crowns.

Many purchasers tend to obtain the largest corms possible in the effort to get the most for their money. With gladiolus, buy high crowned No. 1 size for best results and do not be carried away by the size.

Planting — To insure a succession of bloom coming along from July until frost, make your first planting about the first of May and then plant every two weeks until the middle of June. Do not make the mistake of buying a dozen or two corms and then planting them all at the same time.

The number of days from planting to bloom varies from 60 to 120 days, depending upon the variety. Catalogs usually indicate the number of days to blooming time in brackets immediately after the name of the variety.

Large corms should be planted 4 to 6 inches deep in single rows 2 to 3 feet apart. Set the corms 3 to 6 inches apart in the row, depending upon the size of the corm.

Medium corms should be spaced 2 to 4 inches apart in the row and 2 to 4 inches deep.

The small corms are planted 2 inches apart.

In muck and light sandy soils, the corms are planted 2 inches deeper than in heavy soils to ensure an upright growth. Make sure that the corms are set upright at the time of planting to prevent them from growing outside the row and being damaged by cultivation.

Cultivation is important — Weeds must be eliminated at all costs because they rob the developing gladiolus of much needed food and moisture. For this reason you will have to cultivate the soil thoroughly and frequently. When the plants reach 10 to 12 inches in height, it is a good plan to apply a mulch to the surface of the soil surrounding the planting. This will not only prevent the moisture from evaporating from the soil too quickly, but also hamper the growth of weeds. Make the mulch 3 inches deep in the beginning, anticipating that it will eventually settle down to 1½ to 2 inches. Peat moss, straw, hay, well-rotted barnyard manure, discarded mushroom manure, grass clippings or compost are all suitable mulching materials for gladiolus.

Pest Control — The main insect pest that attacks gladiolus is the "thrip". This is a tiny insect which is hard to see with the human eye, but which does damage out of all proportion to its size by sucking the plant juices from the leaves. You can easily recognize the attacks because the injured leaves will show a silvery streaked condition and the flowers will have a blotched appearance. Best way for the home gardener to control thrips is to spray or dust the leaves and the stems once a week from the time the growth is six inches high until the buds start to open.

Winter storage of gladiolus — About the first week in October the leaves of gladiolus start to turn brown and this is the signal to dig up the corms. It is true that gladiolus will stand a certain amount of frost without harm, but the wisest plan is to get them out of the soil before it becomes wet and messy to handle. You will not be

digging the same corm you planted during the Spring but an entirely new one which formed a month or so after the flowers faded.

Naturally, when digging, you must be careful not to damage the corms, and the best tool for the job is a garden fork. Plan to complete the digging early enough so that the stems will be still firmly attached to the corms.

Each plant will have attached to it one large corm, several smaller corms, and a number of cormels. Before you put your fork into the ground, you will need to decide whether the cormels are to be saved. What are cormels? These are the numerous tiny little bulblets about the size of a garden pea which eventually will grow into a top size gladiolus corm, but it will be at least

two years or more before they flower. The smaller corms will usually give you all the increase in stock you need.

The first step in harvesting gladiolus is the removal of all leaves down to within 2 inches of the soil and this should be done before starting to dig. Twisting or wrenching off the leaves after having dug the plants always does considerable damage to the corm. All foliage removed should be consigned to the home compost heap to help increase the supply of valuable humus for the next year's garden.

Immediately after the corms have been dug, get them into containers and away from the growing area. Even if the day is warm and sunny, get them away from the garden. This is important as it prevents any roving thrips left on the foliage from

Gladiolus in the cut flower garden

getting at or on the corms.

Many home gardeners have discovered that the best containers for storing gladiolus corms are the wooden seedling or fish flats in which you start your annual seeds. You will need a number of these so that each color and variety can be kept separated. Your local fish store is an excellent place to obtain a supply of these wooden fish flats. They are usually only too willing to save a number of them for you.

If possible, dry the freshly dug corms in the sun for a day before storing them in a cool, dry and well aired spot. A frost-free garage, tool or potting shed is the best place to store them for a few weeks before cleaning up for Winter storage. Spread out the corms in the wooden seedling flats where the air can get at them. After two or three weeks they should be thoroughly dry. However, do not go by the length of time, but rather by the fact that the corms will be ready for storing when the old stump of leaves can easily be detached from the new corms.

Having ascertained the corms are thoroughly dry, clean away the old corms, the husks and the stems.

Temperature during storage should be as near 40° as possible, but have no worry if the temperature in your basement goes as high as 50°. It is not necessary to pack the bulbs in peat moss, sand or vermiculite for they store just as well or better without any covering material.

All-America Gladiolus Selections —
Beginners to gardening and the average home gardener will not go wrong if they plant varieties which have been given the coveted All-America award.

The All-America Gladiolus trial gardens are located coast-to-coast, north and south in the United States and Canada, in as wide a variety of soil and climatic conditions as can be imagined.

All our gladiolus hybridists, both amateur and professional, have the privilege of entering their outstanding new originations for consideration by this non-profit organization. Competition is most keen and no award is given lightly. Every variety is rated on these specific points:

Color value
Freedom from short flower heads
Floret form
Substance
Facing and placement

Landmark Gladiolus (top) and Little Pansy (bottom)

Attachment of florets
Freedom of weathering
Opening and keeping qualities
Individuality
Freedom from crooking
Foliage health
Husk and bulb health
Ease of propagation

All-America Gladiolus are sold at uniform low prices by reputable dealers and seedsmen in all parts of the United States and Canada. The corms or bulbs are packaged in bags which bear the variety name, color description, and the plant patent number. Be sure to look for the "All-America Gladiolus Selection" regis-

tered trade mark — it is your assurance of highest quality.

All-America award winners:—

Rusty is the first All-America "smoky". It is really exciting to see it in bloom in the garden for it is beautiful, big, tall and husky. Though a massive variety, the proportions are well balanced and dignified.

The chocolaty red fluted, suede textured florets are formally placed on long spikes and give the effect of a subdued smoky color. At flower shows throughout the United States and Canada, more often than not, the general public seems to respond most enthusiastically to the smoky section.

74

Gypsy Dancer — symbolizes a gay, lively and supple gypsy in a carefree dancing mood. Gracefully ruffled florets on slender stems are colored a vivid scarlet-orange with a sunburst of yellow on the lower petals. This color is fresh and vibrant, spreading throughout the flower as each floret opens. You will find that happy, sparkling Gypsy Dancer is especially valuable for arrangements and makeup work. It makes a fine cut flower and should be extremely popular with gladiolus fanciers everywhere.

China Blue is admired by gladiolus growers. The color of China Blue is a delectable soft blue-violet. It is deeper at the petal tips, then lighter towards the center where a deep violet blotch accents the lower petals. The over-all picture is extremely beautiful with a charm reminiscent of a fragile, antique china vase. Here looks deceive, as the flower has wonderfully heavy substance and is a robust grower.

Landmark — The first impression you get on seeing Landmark in bloom is "This is a knockout". An ethereal glow seems to light its lovely florets, and they fill the eye with their soft creamy brightness.

Landmark has unusual vigor, and its sturdy broad green plants carry extremely well built spikes. Florets are formally placed with precision-like regularity and anywhere from 10 to 14 of the 22 buds will be open at the same time. If there ever was a gladiolus bred for flower show purposes, this is it.

Little Pansy — called the ultimate in flower arrangement material. Everyone admires its velvety deep blue pansy-like blotches which add a distinctive and elegant touch to its light violet colored florets. A nicely proportioned miniature, it grows to a height of 30 to 32 inches and produces early blooming spikes bearing 15 to 18 florets.

Extreme beauty and top notch performance—China Blue

The beautiful deep pink of Maytime

75

Joyous—a joy to see in any garden

somewhat deeper towards the red centers are ruffled and triangular in shape, giving an airy effect. An arrangement of several spikes of Sparkler will make a stunning conversation piece. Of course, it is equally as eyecatching in the garden.

Emperor — This is a wonderful show or exhibition variety. Emperor is of spectacular height and the first time you see it, you will be excited by its striking color, which is regal purple with an ermine white throat. Corms produce tall, majestic spikes with 7 or 8 of its round and recurved florets open at the same time. The plants are usually robust and the spikes consistently tall and straight. Some test gardens have reported it as the tallest variety ever grown, often reaching over 6 feet. This

Joyous — This excellent gladiolus produces elegant beautifully ruffled florets of the formal type. They are colored a rich, brilliant rose which deepens somewhat towards the tip, and as the name suggests they are a joy to see in any garden. Eight or more of the lovely florets are open at the same time, and the plants are healthy and vigorous.

Sparkler — Here is a variety which is as graceful as a butterfly and is a gay combination of yellow and red. The florets, mostly a beautiful, clear yellow shading

Gladiolus come in a wide range of colors

means that in the garden it must be planted to the back of the mixed or annual border.

Apple Blossom — This is a beautiful color, mostly white, with soft pink at the edges of the petals.

Caribbean — A rich deep blue violet, which is particularly striking in glass or pottery vases.

Maytime — This variety is one of the loveliest colors in all the gladiolus world. Gracefully ruffled florets are a deep pure pink, with a white throat. Maytime is an early flower and is ideal for cut flower or exhibition purposes.

Royal Stewart — Its color is a clear light red. The large ruffled flowers are excellently placed on the stems. The plants are vigorous and healthy.

A fine arrangement of Emperor

Caribbean, Royal Stewart, Maytime and Appleblossom

Other recommended varieties

Abu Hassan — Dark violet blue, best in this color.

Ace of Spades — Rich, deep, velvety black red.

Ares — Very pretty flower of pale creamy pink with scarlet blotch.

Catriona — A beautiful deep cream, tall and straight.

Coronation — One of the finest pinks. Clear medium pink with cream throat.

Dark David — Huge flowers of rich maroon.

Dusty Miller — Makes a fine exhibition spike of smoky red.

Elizabeth the Queen — A large ruffled rose lavender.

Ethereal — A very beautiful gladiolus of pale pink and cream.

Fancy — A splendid new light pink. Nicely formed flowers.

77

Rusty and Gypsy Dancer

Friendship—an early ruffled pink Gladiolus

Firebrand — A brilliant new gladiolus of sparkling scarlet. Beautiful, bright flowers.

Fire Opal — A delightful glad of red-orange with yellow throat.

Florence Nightingale — One of the finest whites.

Flower song — Deep golden yellow, large and beautifully ruffled. Has won many prizes.

Flying Dutchman — Grand large florets of pansy blue.

Gold — Nicely ruffled flowers of clear golden yellow.

Green Ice — Grand tall spikes of greenish cream. A most interesting and striking variety.

Irish Rose — An outstanding variety of great beauty. The color is a rich salmon rose enhanced by a lovely greenish tone in the throat.

King David — Tall, red purple. Wonderful spikes.

Leif Erikson — A beautiful creamy white, nicely ruffled. Makes giant spikes and opens 8 to 10 large, wide-open florets.

Mallow — Light rose pink with a creamy throat.

Picardy — Soft shrimp pink. Large and exceptionally fine.

Polygoon — Apricot yellow with light red throat marks.

Quaker Lady — An excellent large flowered variety of rich violet or bluish lavender.

Rajah — Large ruffled red purple.

Ravel — Large and showy flowers of an attractive violet color.

Red Charm — Deep sparkling scarlet, florets large and of fine form.

Red Tape — A big solid red. A real prize winner.

Roseate — A lovely shade of medium rose pink.

Royal Scot — A very fine red toned purple. Makes very good uniform spikes.

Row Bells — Lovely large florets of soft buff pink.

Spotlight—A beautiful dark yellow with a small scarlet red blotch.

Stormy Weather — Salmony pink with lavender gray overcast. Without doubt one of the finest smokies.

Times Square — A beautiful large flowered glad of rich purple.

Uhu — A unique smoky of dusty brown purple.

There is no better cut flower than Gladiolus

Pactolus — Ruffled buff with red throat.

Mary Housley — Cream with red throat.
Corona — White with rose pink edges.
Lavender Prince — Lavender.
Acca Laurentia — Scarlet orange with yellow blotches.
Vink's Glory — Tall, deep yellow.
Cupid — Waxy ruffled white.
Skylark — Orange with yellow throat.
Circe — Deep orange, with large florets.
Spic & Span — Rich ruffled deep pink.

MINIATURE GLADIOLUS

All the miniature gladiolus are proving to be tremendously popular. Nearly all varieties are characterized by densely ruffled, heavy textured florets which stand up well to hot weather. These delightful varieties are the perfect answer for flower arrangements and are much better for planting in beds and borders in the garden than are the tall varieties. They can be extremely attractive if planted in groups of 8 to a dozen between other plants. In the Fall at digging time, they can be easily moved without disturbing the perennials which surround them.

Wax Model — Large florets of blush white. Beautifully ruffled.
Friendship — Early ruffled pink.
Professor Goudrien — Creamy white.
Rose Charm — Bright rose.
Rosa Van Lima — Beautiful clear pink.
Gene — Heavily ruffled light yellow.
Sans Souci — Tall, brilliant scarlet.
Snow Princess — Outstanding white.
Burma — Deep violet, heavily ruffled and fluted deep.
Cover Girl — Tall, salmon pink.
Lantana — Orange buff — cream throat.
Happy End — Light rose.
Bloemfontein — Splendid apricot salmon.

An attractive arrangement of Burma

79

Recommended varieties

Emily's Birthday—This is a miniature whose spikes produce 7 to 8 well placed apricot pink florets with yellowish throats. Since this is one of the earliest of all gladiolus, flowering in less than 60 days, it is proving extremely valuable in areas with short growing seasons.

Corvette — This is the finest scarlet miniature yet introduced. Its tiny flowers are regularly spaced and 19 of them open at once.

Bo-Peep — A buff pink variety with dainty ruffled florets which is also an early bloomer. It is a great favorite for exhibition purposes, since its wide open ruffled florets are well spaced.

White Lace—There seems little doubt that White Lace is the finest white miniature. You will discover its ruffled flowers are exquisite for arrangements.

Bright Eyes — Yellow with red throat. A striking variety which makes very pretty arrangements.

Daintiness — Very heavily ruffled white. For sheer beauty this one tops the list.

Gremlin — A light red with nicely ruffled petals.

Marionette — A heavily ruffled flower of greenish yellow with plum colored throat mark.

Red Button — This a lovely light scarlet. Very pretty and wonderful for arrangements.

Skalawag — Heavily ruffled deep pink with a golden throat.

Toytown — One of the best ruffled miniatures. Rich salmon red with deep golden throat.

Little Gold — Ruffled yellow.
Atom — Fiery scarlet with a white edge.
Crinklette — Orange pink.

Zona — Watermelon pink.
White Butterfly — White and cream.

Corvette—a lovely scarlet miniature

The finest white miniature—White Lace

80

Appleblossom (pink and white), Royal Stewart (red), Maytime (deep pink)

Lilies

"Consider the lilies of the field", is a very familiar quotation from the bible. At the turn of the century, the lilies grown in our gardens were not too much changed from those grown during biblical times. In fact, of the few varieties, there were only two which were well known, the tiger and Easter lilies. Except in the warmer climates, these lilies will not live over from year to year in the garden.

Fortunately, our plant breeders decided to "gild the lily", and their results are a delight to see. We have many new hybrids and varieties with untold variations of soft pastel colors and some now face upwards towards the sun instead of all the flowers pointing down. The beauty and the perfume of the flowers as they open are an exciting experience for anyone. Horticulturists have called the gladiolus the flower of the first half of this century. It seems certain that the lily will be the flower of the second half.

There is no flower grown in the garden which has a longer flowering period than the graceful lilies. By judicious selection of types and varieties it is possible to have a succession of lily bloom in the garden from early June until late September.

Day lily Northstar blooms in mid season

Many home gardeners do not grow lilies because they think they are hard to grow. While it is true they need a little more attention than some of the annuals and vegetables, lilies are certainly not difficult to grow. In fact, the newer hybrids are extremely easy, are virtually all Winter hardy, and may be left in the same site for years.

There are two places in the garden where lilies can be used with a very good purpose. Try planting them in blocks or groups along the rear of the mixed border. Do not plant them singly in a straight line because they will look like soldiers marching in single file. Lilies must be placed in large groups to create a really effective show in the garden. Indeed, they are called "accent flowers".

The other spot where they are truly useful is against the sheltering background provided by a group of evergreens, shrubs or a tall hedge.

In order to ensure a flowering season from June to September, you would have to choose at least six different varieties or classes, and preferably up to 10 or 12. The best planting times for lilies are during October and November, or in April. In the colder areas some difficulty may be experienced with Fall planting because lilies are not ready for shipping until fairly late in the Fall, and freeze-up time may arrive before you are able to obtain them. In such cases you will either have to plant in the Spring, or if the ground shows signs of freezing in the Autumn before you receive the bulbs, keep the locations covered with

Brilliant yellow Meadowlark

Another way of getting good results is to dig the soil 12 inches deep, working the humus into it at the same time, and then getting the extra depth to 18 inches by raising the level of the lily bed some six inches above the surrounding ground level.

A handful of commercial fertilizer for each clump can be mixed into the soil that is to be placed on top of the bulbs.

The depth to plant will depend on the type of lily. Some varieties throw their roots out from the base of the bulb while the majority root from above the bulbs as well as the base. For instance, the Madonna lily, which blooms in June and the Nanking lily

flowering in late June and early July root only from the base of the bulb. On the other hand, most of the new hybrids root from both the stem and the base. When ordering or buying lily bulbs from your dealer, make sure you find out to which group your bulbs belong.

Madonna lilies have to be planted with not more than 1 inch of settled soil over the top of the bulbs, while the stem and base rooting kinds should be covered with not more than 4 inches of soil.

Lilies are sun worshippers needing plenty of sun if they are to grow and flower well. They should be planted in a location where

a mulch 8 or 10 inches deep to prevent the ground from freezing. You can then plant them on the first mild day.

For most areas, Fall planting is definitely best and it will be worth any effort required to get the bulbs into the ground during October and November.

The day you get the bulbs is the day to plant them.

There is one exception to planting late in the Fall. Madonna lilies have to be planted in late August or early September to give them time to form a healthy rosetta of green leaves before the ground freezes solid. These will be evergreen, and cling to the stem of the lily right through the Winter.

Excellent drainage is the most important requirement in growing lilies succesfully. Lilies planted in wet soggy soil would be a complete waste of money. The soil should be porous to let the water drain away easily, and at the same time permit the oxygen to circulate freely through the particles of soil.

This means that before planting you must add a large quantity of humus or organic matter to the soil. The following forms of humus will be satisfactory; peat moss, well-rotted barnyard manure, discarded mushroom manure, materials processed from sewage, or compost.

For reasonably good garden soils use 6 to 8 bushels per 100 square feet, and for poorer soils step up the amount to 8 to 10 bushels. Work the humus into the soil below bulb level. The easiest way of doing this is to dig out the soil in the spot where you are going to plant a clump of lily bulbs down to a depth of 5 inches. Then mix the humus into the next 7 to 10 inches. Digging the soil deeply is one of the big secrets for success in growing lilies.

Good drainage is a must for Lilium Superbum and other types

Superba strain of aurelian hybrid lilies

84

the sun will shine on them until at least two o'clock in the afternoon. Filtered sunlight or semi-shade may bring out the more delicate colors, but this condition tends to make the stems weak and the flowers soft. Although they like plenty of sun, lilies should not be planted near foundation walls, sidewalks or driveways which reflect sunlight or heat.

A most important point to remember about lily bulbs is the fact that they are never completely dormant. This is the reason for replanting them as soon as possible after digging. If slightly limp after their long trip from the bulb grower or dealer, place them in wet peat moss for two or three days. They will soon freshen up and should then be planted immediately. They cannot be treated like tulip or daffodil bulbs which can be dried out and go completely dormant.

Never plant new bulbs where other lilies have failed to grow. There is always a reason for a lily not thriving and this is usually to be found in the soil. The biggest culprit is normally poor drainage, but there also can be a disease problem as well.

Lilies like to have a thick mulch of humus covering the soil surrounding them at all times. The mulch keeps the soil cool, discourages the growth of weeds and eliminates the need for surface cultivation which might hurt the stem roots. Keep the mulch 4 inches deep at all times. To maintain this depth, it will be necessary to add new amounts of humus or organic matter several times during the growing season. Well rotted barnyard manure, peat moss, straw, hay, buckwheat hulls, compost and leaf mold are all satisfactory forms of humus to use. Peat moss being slightly acid is good for lilies and provides an ideal medium for the stem roots when used as a mulch.

Golden Trumpet lilies

Olympic Pink—a blend of pink and fuschia

85

Lilies are sunworshippers needing plenty of sunshine to grow and flower well

In addition to humus you will have to apply a balanced complete fertilizer 3 times during the growing season. Apply it at the rate of a large handful to each clump of lilies, or at 4 pounds per 100 square feet of bed area. Make the first application when the plants are about 5 or 6 inches high and then two further feedings one month apart.

Like all plants lilies need their stems and foliage to build up the bulbs for next year's growth and flowers. This is the reason we should cut the flowers only to prevent them from setting seed, and never cut away any of the foliage. The amount of harm you do in cutting foliage is in direct proportion to

the amount removed. If you cut stems with foliage year after year, you will definitely kill the plant sooner or later.

There are quite a number of lilies which can be grown in pots for summer time blooming around the porch, patio or living-out area. The potted plants can be moved around the garden to places requiring extra color. All the varieties of Speciosum and Aratum lilies are excellent for this purpose and will flower in late July, August and September.

You will need some 5 to 7 inch clay pots, a suitable soil mixture and some broken pieces of clay pot. A suitable potting mix-

ture would consist of two parts good garden soil, one part peat moss or leaf mold and one part sand. Again, the commercial African violet soil mixture is most suitable if you do not wish to make up your own.

The best plan is to pot up the lilies in October or November at the same time as you would plant them outdoors, then sink the pots in a cold frame for the Winter months.

As an added interest, it is very easy to force many lilies in a greenhouse for Winter bloom. The de Graaff mid-century hybrids such as Harmony, Joan Evans and Valencia, and the new yellows, Destiny and Prosperity can be flowered in February and March if potted and put in cold storage or cold frame for six weeks in late Autumn. From then on, the pots should be placed in the sunniest window in the house, or in the greenhouse.

Recommended varieties of the earliest and best.

Coral lily (Pumilum) — This graceful and very fine lily is a native of northeast Asia. Color is an eye-catching sealing-wax scarlet. Several relaxed flowers are produced on each stem which grow from 1 to 2 feet in height. It is a fine variety for cutting and can be easily grown from seed.

Golden Chalice hybrids — Jan de Graaff, the great Oregon lily breeder has introduced an entire new strain of seedlings which show marked improvement over the parent plant. The range of colors varies from clear lemon yellow through the rich warm shades of gold and apricot orange. As with all the de Graaff strains of seedlings, the Golden Chalice hybrids exhibit exceptional vigor. The bulbs are uniformly white, clean and sound. Plant at least 6 inches deep in a warm sunny location in full sun. You will discover the stem roots are heavy and numerous underground stem bulblets are formed. Golden Chalice is extremely drought resistant and so is ideally suited for the warm dry corner of the border where nothing else seems to flourish. Flowering time is June, and the height will vary from 2½ to 4 feet.

Golden Clarion—Golden Clarion is the famous de Graaff strain which has become synonomous with yellow trumpet lilies. Each season it improves in quality and the plants make truly magnificent garden

flowers with their striking golden yellow trumpets. They are a must for every gardener, and will thrive where a Regal lily can be grown. Flowering time is July and they can grow from 4 to 6 feet in height. Some plants have entirely self-colored yellow flowers, while others show distinct wine-red stripes on the reverse of the petals.

Golden Sunburst hybrids — Here we have a remarkable group of vigorous and easy-to-grow lilies which produce up to thirty flowers on their tall stems. Lemon and butter yellow blooms are accented by a rich dark green foliage. These lilies grow to about 6 feet in height and produce their flowers mainly in August. A clump of three will never disappoint you.

Olympic hybrids — This strain is the finest, tallest and largest trumpet lily yet produced. They are a really magnificent group that are extremely beautiful. They have taken over from the old Regal lily because of their broader, stronger flowers, and pyramidal blooming heads. Flowers vary in color from ivory white through soft green, with deeper green and russet tints on the outside of the petals. Flowering time is July and the stems grow from 5 to 7 feet in height.

Olympic Pink — Jan de Graaff has raised tens of thousands of Olympic lilies, and among these he found a few which showed a definite pink color. He intercrossed these rare finds and re-selected the best among their offspring to develop a strain which has a lovely pink color and wonderfully large, wide expanded flowers. The colors are best when these trumpet hybrids can be grown in partial shade, particularly where the sunlight is filtered. They

Golden Clarion—famous yellow trumpet lilies

Graceful Lankongense lilies

87

A pleasing arrangement of lilies with Gladiolus Gold

Destiny—Destiny is a tall, cool and pure lemon-yellow lily. It has just enough delicately placed light brown spots on the petals to afford a beautiful contrast. Destiny opens as many as six large flowers at one time. They are carried well above the lustrous dark green foliage on stems 3 to 4 feet tall.

Red Champion is the lovely Speciosum lily from Japan. It came to Oregon as the gift of the captain of a schooner and was grown in a small farm garden on the slopes of Mt. Hood and it was from that garden Jan de Graaff got his foundation stock. This variety makes a wonderful lily for garden decoration, cut flowers or pot culture in a cool greenhouse. Plants are uniform, disease-free and vigorous. It needs light shade during the hottest part of the day. Flowers in late August and early September at a time when few other lilies are in bloom.

Sentinel — Here we have a pure white strain of Olympic hybrids of great uniformity. These hybrids have outstanding bloom form, widely flaring and being almost bowl shaped. Their coloring is purest white, with soft golden throats and dark brown pollen. Each 5 to 6 foot stem produces a large pyramid-like flower head. Up to 20 blooms will be produced in July.

Jillian Wallace—Here we have perhaps the most striking and famous hybrid introduced in recent years. Neither words nor photographs can really do it justice. Roy Wallace of Australia did the hybridizing, and named the resulting new variety after his granddaughter. The blooms are large and measure 7 to 10 inches across. Their color is a rich carmine red, with white, somewhat wavy petal margins, and deep crimson spots. This lily is beautifully scented, has broad dark green leaves, and flowers in August.

The Palmer hybrids — Prior to World War II, Doctor Frank Palmer of Vineland, Ontario had tremendous success in breeding new gladiolus.

After many years of careful, painstaking work, Dr. Palmer has given us an excellent series of July and August flowering lilies. They are strong, reliable growers, and add masses of new color to the garden in the hot, dry months.

need a cool, moist well-drained soil, but are vigorous in most locations.

Ruby—This is a beautiful variety that should be in every garden. This clump-forming hybrid has upright blooms a deep ruby red in color. In fact, the red is so intense that it flashes color for great distances. The rich color of the flowers is framed by dark green foliage. The sturdy stems are low-growing, reaching about 2 feet in height. It will grow well in full sun, partial shade, and in a variety of soils. It is truly a joy to see it in flower in the June and July garden.

Enchantment—A most beautiful, most vibrantly colored new hybrid lily. The many large, cup-shaped, upright flowers of an intense glaring nasturtium-red, lights up the garden making it visible from far away. You will find the flowers are unusually

long lasting, starting to appear in late June and carrying on until about the middle of July.

Redbird is a Palmer hybrid of great quality. The mature stems grow up to 5 feet in height, carrying large outward-facing flowers measuring 5 inches across. Color is a lively red, well displayed by rich green foliage. Redbird is fine for mixing with other garden perennials or white flowered annuals. Blooming time is the last three weeks of July.

Valiant is another one of these excellent Palmer hybrids. We cannot recommend this lily too highly. Season after season it delights all visitors and wins hundreds of new friends around the world. In mid-July the slightly upward tilting flowers open and continue well into August because of the valuable secondary buds. We are not exaggerating when we say it produces numerous blooms, because you will get up to 35 on some stems. Color is a deep and lustrous ruby red, and the stems grow 3 to 5 feet high. The glossy green leaves make a remarkable contrast with the flowers. This is an easy variety to grow in full sun or partial shade.

Meadowlark is the creation of J. C. Taylor of the Department of Horticulture at the Ontario Agricultural College. This is the first in a series of yellow seedlings. The brilliant yellow flowers have chocolate spots and are upward facing. Meadowlark starts to flower about July 10th and continues until early August. This lily has already won lots of attention and a number of important awards.

The Temple hybrids form a new group of trumpet lilies developed through many years of breeding and selection by John Shaver of Oregon. The vigorous free-flowering stems grow from 4 to 6 feet or more in height. They are excellent for planting in groups in full sun or partial shade. Blooms

are fragrant and are produced in quantity in July.

Sun Temple—Features clean, light yellows to warm golden tones of great clarity and brightness. Sometimes the exteriors are flushed with olive or wine shades. Plants are vigorous, producing luxuriant foliage and strong stems.

Amethyst Temple — Produces massive trumpets in exciting shades of amethyst pink to deep columbine red. Pink and reddish trumpet lilies are in tremendous demand and these recent newcomers should prove most welcome in any garden. In warmer sections of the country it may be wise to try some partial shade and a good ground

mulch to help preserve the deep colorings of the flower as very hot sunlight tends to fade the blooms. These are wonderful for cutting, flower arrangements, or in the garden. Blooms are carried on stems 5 to 7 feet in height.

Jade Temple — Pale moonlight greens and lime whites distinguish these large, graceful trumpets. The flower throats are greenish yellow or white with green or brown exteriors. You will find their cool coloring is most refreshing in the heat of Summer. They feature the typical fragrance and vigor of the trumpet hybrids.

Martagon Album—This dainty lily was found growing in the mountains of Dal-

The delightful summer flowering Ismene

matia and is a true white colored lily with dainty wax-like flowers. These are gracefully spaced on 4 foot stems which carry a warm green foliage. Home gardeners like it not only for its beauty, but also for the fact that it flowers in June. It is so easy to grow it could be called the beginner's lily. Bulbs will increase from year to year, forming larger and larger spikes.

Harlequin hybrids — This is a new, very hardy hybrid strain coming in colors that vary from ivory white through lilac, and old rose to violet and purple, with shades of salmon, terra cotta and amber pink. Mature plants will carry from 12 to 15 flowers, all fully recurved on 5 foot stems. Harlequin hybrids flower in June.

Paisley hybrids—This strain of hybrid lilies of great beauty, sports all the lovely colors of the well-known Paisley shawls. The flowers are recurved and range from ivory white through yellow and orange, lilac and tangerine to mahogany. Each flower is accented with tiny maroon dots. These beautiful lilies flower in June. They may take a year to settle in, but once established will grow vigorously and multiply quite rapidly. Unlike most lilies they prefer a neutral soil and can even stand some lime.

Bellingham hybrids—A hybrid strain of lilies raised from native species of the United States West Coast. The flowers are ideally spaced on tall, slender straight stems that are particularly long lasting. Each pyramidal flower head produces up to 20 blooms. They may be cut as the first buds open and will remain fresh until the entire spike is in bloom. The color range is complete from clear yellow through the yellow-oranges to bright orange red with scarlet tipped petals. Most of the flowers are intensely spotted with brown or reddish brown. The Bellingham hybrids are ideal for partial or light shade. Be sure and leave the bulbs undisturbed since they divide and branch rapidly to form large clumps. A Winter mulch is recommended in the colder sections to protect the bulbs against alternate thawing and freezing.

Cascade Madonna lily — A startling improvement on the oldest known cultivated garden plant. One of the big features of this new variety is its high resistance to disease. The foliage stays green long after the flowers have faded. The Cascade Madonna lily, like the others of this family, flowers

in June at the same time as delphiniums and they make a particularly fine show in the mixed border when planted together in clumps.

Cascade White Elf — Here we have a charming dwarf variety never over 14 inches tall. It produces pure white flowers which are a perfect miniature of the tall Cascade Madonnas. This is the first dwarf Madonna lily variety ever offered. They of course need planting shallow like all Madonnas, with not more than 1 inch of soil over the top of the bulbs. Flowering time is the same as the taller growing varieties.

Preston Hybrids—Miss Isabella Preston, was one of the great ornamental plant breeders of this century.

Addington is one of her lovely hybrids that has won awards and attention everywhere. The large blooms are a most attractive yellow, are cup shaped and chocolate spotted. They are carried on well spaced flower heads.

Brenda Watts—Another Preston hybrid which deserves a place in every garden. The strong 4 to 6 foot stems bear grenadin red reflexed flowers.

Midwest Majesty grows 4 feet tall

90

Dahlias

B.C.—a popular dahlia for cutting

Helen Stafford

Arthur Godfrey

DAHLIAS—The dahlia is a very husky and colorful flower that is reaching new heights in popularity. It can be used for almost any spot in the garden. The modern dahlia comes in a wide variety of forms. Sizes range from the dwarf types growing from 1 foot to 1½ feet in height to tall giants that grow 6 to 8 feet tall. There are intermediate kinds which grow 3 to 4 feet in height, these include the semi-cactus varieties which are hard to beat for cut flower purposes. In fact, unless you grow the dwarf types which are excellent for massing in beds, the chief use of the dahlia is for cut flower or show purposes.

The most important requirement for dahlias is that they must be located where they will receive sunshine 80 to 100% of the time. They prefer a soil which is rich and fertile. We say a soil is fertile when it contains plenty of humus and lots of plant food. Whether your soil is light or heavy you treat it in the same way. First of all, scatter over it a quantity of humus or organic material. For very poor soils it is necessary to add 10 bushels per 100 square feet; for soils in reasonable condition which will grow vegetables, 6 bushels per 100 square feet will be sufficient. The complete fertilizer is added at the same time at the rate of 4 pounds per 100 square feet. Thoroughly mix the humus, the fertilizer and the soil together, either by digging by hand or if space permits you could use a rotary tiller.

Planting time for dahlias in most areas is around the first of June. There is no point in planting them earlier, otherwise you will have them attempting to burst into flower when the weather is too hot. For all but the very dwarf varieties, do not plant your dahlia tubers any closer than 3 feet.

When planting time does come along, dig the planting hole at least 18 inches deep. If your soil tends to be soggy and wet during a rainy season, place two inches of small pebbles in the bottom of the hole to facilitate drainage. Next, take some good top soil, enough to add about 6 inches of soil to the hole. In this top soil, mix one rounded tablespoonful of complete fertilizer and a quantity of humus. Add this soil mixture and then on top of it place enough good top soil, without fertilizer, to bring the level of the soil up to the required planting depth of 8 inches.

Next, place the tuber firmly in the loose soil, with the eye facing upwards. A 5 to 6 foot stake should be placed at the side of the tuber and next to the eye, before the tuber is covered in with soil. This will prevent danger of injury to the tuber and the root system which easily occurs when an attempt is made to place a stake after the tuber has been covered.

Do not fill in the soil completely at the time of planting as you would with a shrub or evergreen. Merely add a couple of inches of good top soil at planting time and as the plants grow the soil is gradually placed around the growing stems until the holes are filled.

Mulching is good practice with dahlias. A mulch will eliminate the need for further cultivation and will aid in keeping the soil moist and cool. A 2 or 3 inch layer of mulch extending out for some distance from the plant will do the job to perfection. Any humus material, such as discarded mushroom manure, well rotted barnyard manure, peat moss, compost or materials processed from sewage will be highly satisfactory.

91

After the plants have developed several sets of leaves, pinch off the tops, just above the second set of leaves. Simply pinch out the leading tip of the shoot, between the forefinger and the thumb. This will force the plants to bush out and produce four strong branches. After pinching, when the plants are about 12 inches high, give them a feeding with a complete fertilizer by using one rounded tablespoonful for each plant. Make sure the fertilizer is worked into the surrounding soil.

Once the dahlias have reached two feet in height, it is time to start tying them loosely to the stake with raffia or prepared plant ties.

Dahlias are half-hardy plants which have to be dug and stored before the really hard frosts arrive. Time to do this is just as soon as the first heavy frosts have blackened the leaves and stems of the dahlia plants. This is a warning sign to get them out of the ground.

The first step is to cut off all the stems and foliage at the ground level. Do not burn or throw this away in the garbage — place it in your home compost heap to help your garden another year. On the other hand if the foliage or the tubers are diseased, consign them to the fire heap. There is no profit in carrying over-weak and diseased plants; it is far better to destroy them and obtain new plants later.

La Gioconda—an exciting red and green dahlia from France

The way you lift dahlias is most important as beneath the surface of the soil they are composed of fleshy underground stems or tubers which can be easily broken or cut. The best way is to first make a cut with a spade or digging fork completely around the plant and far enough out from the stem so there will be no danger of damaging the tubers. Then start levering or gently prying with the spade or fork until the clump easily lifts out of the ground leaving considerable soil clinging to the tubers. Be sure to handle the clump gently to prevent breakage at the neck. Tubers broken away at the neck are rarely any good another year. Try to lift the clumps of dahlias on a warm sunny day.

Turn the clumps over to allow the sun to dry the soil and before evening comes move them under cover. If left out overnight they are liable to be damaged by frost.

The ideal storage place is a cool dry cellar where the Winter temperature is between 40 to 45 degrees. The vegetable and fruit storage cupboards built in basements is suitable for storing dahlias. If this type of storage is available, or if you can store them in a basement that is cool, dry and where the Winter temperature is between 40 and 45 degrees then leave as much soil as possible on the plants. On the other hand,

if the storage is damp or the temperature rises above 50 degrees, then all the soil should be removed, and the tubers dried thoroughly before storing them in a box of dry sand. In any case, do not put them away and forget to examine them from time to time during the Winter. By checking once in a while you will be able to see if they are keeping in good condition — if not you can take steps to remedy the situation.

Classes of dahlias

The two large-flowered classes of dahlias are the informal and the formal decorative. There is really not too much difference between these two classes and both their flowers are fully double. The formal decoratives, as you might gather from the name, have large, broad, stiff petals, and the colors are in somewhat regular arrangement. The informal decoratives, on the other hand, have ruffled or twisted ends, giving a more informal appearance.

The flowers of both classes can vary from 8 to 12 inches in diameter. Neither type is used as a cut flower.

For the cut flower garden, it would be hard to find anything better than the cactus, or semi-cactus types of dahlias. Again, both types have fully double flowers with the petals of the cactus being straighter and stiffer than those of the semi-cactus.

The flowers of each class average 7 to 8 inches in diameter.

Miniature dahlias comprise all those which normally produce flowers that do not exceed 4 inches in diameter, excluding the pom pom class.

Pompom dahlias have fully double flowers which are ball shaped or slightly flattened and the flowers measure 2 to 3 inches in diameter. For exhibiting at flower shows you would not be able to use those over 2 inches in diameter.

Recommended varieties

Code: (F.D.) — Formal decorative
    (I.D.) — Informal decorative
    (S.C.) — Semi-cactus
    (C.) — Cactus

Arthur Godfrey (F.D.) — Enormous flower of orient red with buff shadings. One of the largest of all dahlias.

Avalon (F.D.)—Beautiful clear yellow. Favors cold weather.

Helen Stafford (I.D.)—A lovely white and pink variety from England.

B.C. (S.C.) — One of the most popular dahlias for cutting, whose color is an excellent combination of rose and yellow.

Five Star General (F.D.)—Very large, light amaranth pink with tips of soft maize yellow.

Gertrude Britten (F.D.) — Excellent garden variety bearing large flowers of bright red.

Jean Kerr (F.D.) — The most popular white. Exceptional keeping quality.

The Cardinal (S.C.)—An extra fine red dahlia.

Pape's Yellow (C.)—An excellent garden dahlia which makes a fine cut flower.

Mrs. James Albin (F.D.)—Soft lemon yellow, strong bush producing excellent cut flowers.

Ogden Reid (F.D.)—The finest, largest, pink blooming dahlia. Most dependable.

Pape's Yellow

Red and White (F.D.)—A consistently good bicolor. Red base with white tips.

Jane Cowl (I.D.)—Large shaggy flower of copper and gold.

Madonna (I.D.)—Color is bright lemon yellow. Flowers held high above foliage on long, stiff stems. Very profuse.

Watchung Giant (I.D.) — A huge yellow gold variety that is a constant performer for garden use.

White Wonder (I.D.) — A beauty for garden display with large flowers of pure white and perfect from one strong stem.

World's Event (I.D.) — Large tyrian rose flowers on vigorous healthy bushes.

Berger's Masterpiece (C)—Color is a soft lavender-pink with a yellow base. Narrow incurved florets borne profusely on tall wiry stems.

Blijheid (C)—Pure bright orange, perfect forms.

Michigan White (S.C.) — Many perfectly shaped white flowers borne on long, strong stems.

Scarlet Leader (C)—Perfect flowers of cactus type hold their bright scarlet color in brightest sunshine.

Silvretta (C) — Lilac salmon-rose flowers medium size but borne in great abundance.

White Superior (C)—Large pure white cactus with perfect form and excellent growth habits.

Miniature dahlias

Bishop of Llandorf—Attractive bright scarlet flower with bronze foliage.

Blue Eye — Formal lavender-pink with dark center.

La Giaconda — An exciting red and green dahlia from France.

Ike—Rich red, very profuse.

Peggy Lindley—Clear golden orange.

Sandra—Red and white formal bicolor.

Gold Coin

White Fawn—Without doubt the finest decorative white variety. Extremely free flowering.

Pom Pom dahlias

Albino—Small flowers of pure white.

Amber Queen—Solid amber color.

Rhonda — A lovely lavender pompom from Australia.

Little Herman—A red and white pom pom.

Mary Munns—Fine lavender variety.

Morning Mist—Rosy-lavender overlay on white base.

Yellow Gem—Creamy yellow.

Summer Flowering Bulbs

Ranunculus

Not many people realize that there are a large group of Summer flowering bulbs which not only provide delightful beauty for your garden, but in many cases will give you flowers which few of your neighbours will be growing. Not every bulb dealer carries any or all of these bulbs so you may have to do a little searching, but the results in your garden will more than make up for any extra trouble on your part.

MONTEBRETIAS

There will be few gardens anywhere in which you will see montebretias growing. This is a Summer flowering bulb that requires about the same treatment as gladiolus. It needs to be planted in full sun and the soil should contain plenty of humus. The bulbs have to be planted four inches deep and 5 inches apart. Unfortunately, they are not hardy anywhere in the North and so will need taking up in the Fall, just like gladiolus, and storing in the same manner.

A check through your bulb dealer's catalog will reveal some beautiful hybrids which are really worth growing. The long panicles of bloom come in rich colors of copper, yellow, red and orange. Planting time will be the same as for gladiolus in your area. About the only major pest that attacks montebretias is the pesky thrip. Dusting or spraying the plants every week with an all-purpose insecticide will keep insect pests under reliable control.

RANUNCULUS—This very fine flowering tuber is widely grown by florists, but not too many home gardeners realize that they are also desirable garden flowers. The plants grow up to 1½ feet in height from tuberous roots. They produce very many double globe-like yellow, orange, scarlet, crimson, pink or white blooms on graceful long stems. Combined with anemones or planted alone in a spot where they can be easily seen, ranunculi make a fine show of color in any garden.

They like the soil to contain plenty of humus and thrive the best in a location which provides full sun.

Planting time is early Spring, just as soon as the soil can be worked. Set the tubers 2 inches deep and 6 inches apart. It should not be long before you will have a very good source of spectacular and decorative cut flowers.

TIGRIDIAS or MEXICAN SHELL-FLOWERS — Here we have a very easily grown Summer-flowering bulb whose showy flowers last but a day, but several open in succession on each of the 1½ to 2 foot flowering stems. Each flower measures 3 to 4 inches across and is composed of three wide-spreading flared petals set off by three smaller ones. They have a large spotted cup-like center and the colors are buff, yellow, orange and flame-red.

Because of their size and brilliant colors, groups of tigridias make fine flashes of color in the mixed border and foundation planting. They can be cut when in bud because the flowers open readily after the stems are placed in water.

Culture is just about the same as for gladiolus. Start planting them during May and make two or three plantings ten days apart. Set the corms 2 to 3 inches deep and 8 inches apart. They will need digging in the Fall at the same time as the gladiolus.

Be sure and give them a position in the garden where they will get full sun all the time.

GALTONIA (Summer hyacinth)—This lovely Summer hyacinth is a tender bulb which lends dignity and beauty to the Summer border. Once the delphiniums are through blooming, or in some cases even before they have stopped flowering, the galtonias will already be starting to bloom. In July and early August each bulb produces flowering spikes which average three to four feet in height. Along the upper part of each spike are produced many nodding pure white bells. For large cut flower arrangements, it is hard to find anything to equal these fine Summer blooming bulbs.

Tigridia

Planting time is the 24th of May, or after the last frost. They need planting 5 to 6 inches deep and 8 inches apart. Galtonias do not thrive well in poor soil so be sure to give them a generous feeding of humus and complete fertilizer before planting. They will grow much better if given a location in full sun.

Like the montebretia, they will need digging in the early Fall and storing over Winter indoors.

PERUVIAN DAFFODIL — Here we have another delightful and not very well known Summer blooming bulb, which carries the rather delightful name of Peruvian daffodil. It produces large, fragrant, lily-like blossoms which are most unusual to say the least. The flowers grow 4 inches across and the spikes of bloom last a long time after cutting.

The Peruvian daffodil is a good plant for interesting children in gardening because the spikes of bloom spring up very fast after planting. Sometimes the buds appear in just two or three weeks. It will be no use setting the bulbs on poorly drained soil, and it should contain a large quantity of humus and fertilizer. The planting depth is 4 to 5 inches. To maintain a succession of bloom, you will have to make 3 or 4 plantings 10 days apart.

Unlike many plants, the Peruvian daffodil is extremely decorative when not in flower. The foliage is attractive in the garden, and is also very useful for flower arrangements. In the Fall, the bulbs should be dug before frost and stored indoors.

ACIDANTHERA—This member of the Iris family is an excellent Summer flowering bulb. Its flowering time is mid-Summer when it produces 5 to 6 butterfly-like flowers per stalk. The blossoms are fragrant, and open in succession over a period of two or more weeks. Foliage is quite like gladiolus, but it is much more handsome. The flowers are a delicate white, fragrant and have maroon colored centers. The grace and beauty of these flowers makes them excellent for cutting. Another important point in their favor is the fact that they can be cut while in bud, and will still open readily.

Their culture in the garden is the same as for gladiolus. Prepare the soil in exactly the same way as we suggested for the galtonias.

Time to plant is any time during May setting them 3 inches deep and 6 inches apart in the rows.

LYCORIS (SQUAMIGERA) or MAGIC LILY OF JAPAN—This is an old garden favorite which is seldom if ever grown now in the garden. It is extremely hardy and long lived, and having flowers which suddenly appear in late July or August. The bulbs are usually delivered some time in August or early September and should be planted in a partially shady location where the soil is rich and contains plenty of humus.

Best location for this magic lily of Japan is in front of evergreens or shrubs which will form a background for the three foot stems. After planting, you will not see any more of this late Summer flowering bulb until early Spring when handsome green leaves will start growing rapidly out of the ground and eventually reach a height of 2 to 2½ feet. These quickly reach maturity then die away and disappear completely.

Around the first week in August the flower spikes start coming through the soil and grow rapidly. Within a week or ten days they will have grown to three feet in height and start to produce clusters of mauve pink lily-like flowers which give forth a delicate fragrance.

Once planted, it is possible you will not have to move them in your lifetime. Indeed, you will harm them if you move them.

Montebretias require about the same treatment as Gladiolus

ANEMONES (DECAEN AND ST. BRIGID)

ANEMONES (DECAEN AND ST. BRIGID)—Despite their rich coloring and large size exotic blooms these fine garden flowers are not difficult to grow. The colors range from purple, blue, red, rose to white. The blossoms will be as much as 3 to 4 inches in diameter on stems growing 18 inches tall.

Anemones are very effective when planted in good size blocks in the rock garden, at the front of the foundation planting or mixed border. They also make superb cut flowers.

They are not too particular about soil conditions, although there is no doubt that they do best in a sandy loam. No matter what soil you have in your garden, it should contain plenty of humus. Anemones prefer a location where they will get morning sun only. A foundation bed on the east side of the house would be an ideal location. Plant them 2 inches deep and 12 inches apart, just as soon as the soil is workable in the early Spring. It is unfortunate that they are not reliably hardy in the colder areas, so they will have to be dug up in the Fall and replanted the next Spring, or fresh bulbs will have to be set out every Spring.

In the warmer climates they will come up every year and flower without ever being disturbed.

OXALIS—Here we have a pleasing little bulbous flower you can grow outdoors or in the house. For many years its low shamrock-shaped foliage and rose or white buttercup type blooms produced on long trailing stems have made it a popular favorite. The oxalis is used for edging the front of the border or foundation bed in the Summer or for a hanging basket in a sunny window in the Winter. It will flower for weeks on end.

For Summer bloom outdoors, plant the little bulbs one inch deep and 6 inches apart. They like a sandy loam and should not be planted until after the last frost. In most areas this would be from the 15th to the 20th of May.

In the Autumn, when flowering has ceased and the foliage has matured you dig and store as for any of the other Summer flowering bulbs. One thing is certain at that time, you will find many more bulbs than you planted. There is hardly any bulb that increases more rapidly.

Anemones in all but the warmer climates should be planted in early Spring